Second Edition

INVITING SCHOOL SUCCESS

A Self-Concept Approach
to Teaching and Learning

William Watson Purkey
University of North Carolina at Greensboro

John M. Novak
Brock University

Wadsworth Publishing Company
Belmont, California
A Division of Wadsworth, Inc.

Education Editor: Bob Podstepny

Production Editor: Deborah M. Oren

Designer: Detta Penna

Copy Editor: Judith Hibbard

Cover Designer: Grant Peterson

Cover Photo: © Elizabeth Crews/Stock, Boston

Printed in the United States of America

8 9 10—89

Acknowledgments

The excerpt on page 79 is reprinted with permission of Macmillan Publishing Co., Inc. and
Jonathan Cape Ltd. from *Manchild in the Promised Land* by Claude Brown. Copyright © 1965 by
Claude Brown.

The excerpt on pages 80–81 is reprinted with permission of Allyn & Bacon, Inc. from *Helping
Relationships: Basic Concepts for the Helping Professions* by A. Combs, D. Avila, and W. Purkey,
Allyn & Bacon, Inc., 1971.

The excerpt on pages 13–14 is reprinted with permission of E. P. Dutton & Co., Inc. and Curtis
Brown Limited from *Nigger: An Autobiography* by Dick Gregory, with Robert Lipsyte. Copyright © 1964 by Dick Gregory Enterprises, Inc.

Library of Congress Cataloging in Publication Data

Purkey, William Watson
      Inviting school success.

      Bibliography: p.
      Includes index.
      1. Teaching.   2. Teacher-student relationships.
3. Motivation in education.   I. Novak, John M.
II. Title.
LB1025.2.P89   1984   371.1'02   83-6954
ISBN 0-534-02891-8

ISBN 0-534-02891-8

This book is dedicated to

Cynthia Purkey Gaines
Linda Novak
Natalie Tara Novak
Imogene Hedrick Purkey
William Watson Purkey, Jr.

whose presence invites a celebration in our hearts.

CONTENTS

Preface   xi

Preface to the First Edition   xiii

Chapter One: Introduction to Invitational Education   1

  What Is Invitational Education?   2

  The Development of Invitational Education   3

  Life in and around Schools   4

    Teacher Expectancies   5
    Student Attitudes   6

  Professional Efficacy   7

    The Cumulative Effect of Experience   7
    The Importance of Consistency   7

  Patterns of Communication   8

    Feeling Invited   8
    Feeling Disinvited   10
    Labeling and Grouping   11
    Negative Messages   13

  Importance of the Inviting Approach   15

  Levels of Functioning   16

    Level One: Intentionally Disinviting   17
    Level Two: Unintentionally Disinviting   18
    Level Three: Unintentionally Inviting   18
    Level Four: Intentionally Inviting   19

  Summary   20

Chapter Two: Foundations of Invitational Education   *21*

   The Perceptual Tradition   *22*

       Behavior Is Based on Perceptions   *23*
       Perceptions Are Learned   *24*
       Perceptions Can Be Reflected Upon   *25*

   Self-Concept Theory   *25*

       Self-Concept Development   *26*
       Self-Concept as Guidance System   *29*
       Significance of Positive Self-Regard   *32*

   Summary   *34*

Chapter Three: The Inviting Approach   *35*

   Teacher Perception   *36*

       Viewing Students as Able   *38*
       Perceiving Students as Valuable   *39*
       Seeing Students as Responsible   *40*
       Viewing Oneself Positively   *42*
       Perceiving Education Affirmatively   *43*

   Teacher Stance   *44*

       Intentionality   *45*
       Respect   *45*
       Direction   *46*
       Responsibility   *46*

   Teacher Behavior   *47*

       To Send or Not to Send   *48*
       To Accept or Not to Accept   *49*

   An Inviting Approach to Discipline   *50*

   Summary   *53*

Chapter Four: Inviting Skills   *55*

   Being Ready   *56*

Preparing the Environment   *56*
Preparing Oneself   *57*

Being With   *58*

Developing Trust   *58*
Reaching Each Student   *60*
Reading Situations   *62*
Making Invitations Attractive   *64*
Ensuring Delivery   *65*
Negotiating   *66*
Handling Rejection   *67*

Following Through   *69*

Summary   *70*

Chapter Five: The Person in the Process   *71*

Being Personally Inviting with Oneself   *72*

Being Personally Inviting with Others   *74*

Being Professionally Inviting with Oneself   *76*

Being Professionally Inviting with Others   *77*

Relating   *78*
Asserting   *81*
Investing   *83*
Coping   *85*

Summary   *87*

Chapter Six: Two Models for Tomorrow's Schools   *89*

The Efficient Factory   *90*

Mass Production   *91*
Uniform Product   *91*
Cost Effectiveness   *91*
Technology   *91*
Centralized Control   *92*
Workers as Functionaries   *92*

The Efficient Factory School   92

> Mass Production   93
> Uniform Product   93
> Cost Effectiveness   93
> Technology   93
> Centralized Control   94
> Workers as Functionaries   94

The Inviting Family   94

> Respect for Individual Uniqueness   95
> Cooperative Spirit   95
> Sense of Belonging   95
> Pleasing Habitat   95
> Positive Expectations   96

The Inviting Family School   96

> Respect for Individual Uniqueness   96
> Cooperative Spirit   96
> Sense of Belonging   97
> Pleasing Habitat   97
> Positive Expectations   97

Conclusion   98

Appendix A: Inviting School Success   101

What Elementary-School Teachers Can Do   102

What Food-Service Professionals Can Do   105

What Middle-School Teachers Can Do   107

What Physical Educators Can Do   110

What School Administrators Can Do   113

What School Bus Drivers Can Do   117

What School Counselors Can Do   119

What School Secretaries Can Do   123

What Secondary-School Teachers Can Do   126

Appendix B: Inviting and Disinviting Signals   131

Verbal Comments   132

Personal Behaviors   133

Physical Environments   134

Printed Signs   135

References   136

Index   154

PREFACE

This second edition of *Inviting School Success* intends to capture the recent theoretical developments and practical applications that have appeared since the publication of the first edition. Thus, the second edition is simultaneously more abstract and more concrete than the first.

In writing this second edition we could empathize with Pogo, who commented, "We are surrounded with insurmountable opportunities." Invitational education is developing faster than we can write these ideas on paper.

The rapid growth of invitational education has resulted largely from the contributions made by professionals in many fields throughout the United States and Canada. Thanks to dissertations, research papers, symposia, reports, workshop presentations, and countless formal and informal interactions with friends and colleagues, the concepts and strategies that appear in this second edition have emerged.

Any real revision of a book comes from a revised understanding and a deeper appreciation of fundamental ideas. In revising *Inviting School Success,* we came to realize that although "teaching is inviting," *everyone* and *everything* in and around schools serve as signal systems that invite or disinvite success in school. Thus, this book provides an approach to education that has a much wider focus and application than is found in other approaches to teaching and learning.

The opening chapters of the second edition present the nature and foundations of invitational education. These chapters present an overview of the perceptual tradition and an introduction to self-concept theory that explain the dynamics involved in becoming professionally inviting.

The middle chapters provide a close look at invitational education and present some systematic strategies for skill development. Three basic skills are emphasized to answer the question, "How does one function in a dependably inviting manner?"

The closing chapters of the second edition of *Inviting School Success* emphasize the importance of orchestrating four areas of functioning: (1) being personally inviting with oneself, (2) being personally inviting with others, (3) being professionally inviting with oneself, and (4) being professionally inviting with others. Our book ends with a vision of what we see as the school of tomorrow.

To provide additional strategies for professionals in the field, an appendix is included that offers several hundred examples of ways to make schools more personally and professionally inviting. These examples are listed under nine professional helping roles. A second appendix provides lists of inviting and disinviting signals found in and around schools. We see these as simply illustrative of the countless opportunities available for making a school "the most inviting place in town."

Although it would be impossible to thank everyone who has contributed to this second edition of *Inviting School Success,* their contributions are deeply appreciated. Among the many professionals from education, nursing, counseling, administration, food service, and related fields that we wish to thank there are those who deserve a special recognition. These are Al Bennett, Gary Chandler, Dorothy Crissman, Vic Cicci, Dean Fink, Tim Gerber, Gail Heald-Taylor, Hal and Cathy Hillgren, Lisa Hockaday, Lynn Horton, Charlotte Lambeth, Jim Love, Don McBrien, Rebecca Miller, Jack Murphy, Marcia Nahikian, Hank Petkau, Venus Pinnix, Don and Dorothy Russell, Virada Schuessler, Mary Margaret Snyder, William Stafford, Judy Stillion, Brent Tremblay, Robert Turner, Bruce Voelkel, Jim Wagner, Terri Warren, Dick Warters, and Al Wheeler.

We are also grateful to Nancy N. Loposer, Auburn University; Eldon M. Drake, Utah State University; and Carlos J. Vallejo, Arizona State University, whose reviews helped to further refine this second edition.

These friends are among the many who have contributed to invitational education. We can "no other answer make but thanks, and thanks, and ever thanks" (Shakespeare, *Twelfth Night,* Act III, Scene ii).

PREFACE TO THE FIRST EDITION

Several years ago I wrote a book that explored the positive, persistent relationship between various dimensions of self-concept and school achievement (*Self-Concept and School Achievement,* Englewood Cliffs, N.J.: Prentice-Hall, 1970). That earlier book presented research-based evidence to support the thesis that each student's subjective, personal evaluation of his or her unique existence significantly relates to the student's success or failure in school. Although conclusions remain tentative (it is risky to assume simple causal relationships in an interrelated, open system), the research emerging since 1970 continues to support my original thesis.

Following the appearance of the earlier book, many people contacted me to ask such questions as: "Assuming that self-concept does play an important role in school achievement, how can we build a student's self-concept?" "What can our school do to enhance students' self-esteem?" "What can we do to make self-concept an important part of our school curriculum?" In response to these questions, I have written this book, *Inviting School Success.*

Inviting School Success approaches its subject from a humanistic viewpoint. Compared with other approaches to teaching that view teachers as managers, motivators, shapers, researchers, consultants, counselors, or guides, this approach defines the teacher as *inviter.* This book describes good teaching as the process of inviting students to see themselves as able, valuable, and self-directing and of encouraging them to act in accordance with these self-perceptions.

Rather than viewing students as physical objects to be moved about like puppets on strings, the teacher's primary role is seeing students in essentially positive ways and inviting them to behave accordingly. Students, like all of us, greatly benefit from others who see and communicate to them the positive traits and potentials that they may not see in themselves. "In my junior year of high school," a student wrote, "my favorite teacher and I engaged in a discussion about the girls and boys most likely to be nominated for student council president. My choices were two of my very good friends. The teacher and I agreed that my two friends were highly qualified, but then she asked 'And what about you?' I remember thinking this was hilarious; I couldn't picture me in that role. Still, she insisted that I had the same qualities as my friends. Much later, she told me she was not a bit surprised when I was elected student council president." Invitations, as we will see, bid us to grow and to realize our human potential.

At this point, we cannot guarantee that students will learn more or be happier in an inviting school environment. However, research on invitational teaching (teaching that corresponds with the model presented in this book) has begun (Inglis, 1976; Purkey, 1975, 1976a, 1976b). This research, plus the anecdotal reports of over two thousand students at various grade levels, reveal that what students remember about "good teachers" are the invitations to learning sent by these teachers. What they remember about "bad teachers" are the ways these teachers disinvited students. "It's terrible," wrote one fourth-grader, "when Mrs. Reed is picking on me, and everything is missing, and tears are rolling down my eyes." Judging by what we now know about school life, an invitational approach to education very likely increases the probability of student success and happiness in the classroom.

Because this book stresses the importance of school success, it may be viewed as advocating a "basics approach" to education. Such a view is correct insofar as it emphasizes the importance of academic achievement. At the same time, the invitational approach is anchored in an unconditional commitment to the value, ability, and self-directing powers of the individual student. In light of a growing emphasis on the *factory model* of education characterized by a mechanistic orientation—the view of students and teachers as functionaries, with a primary emphasis on product—the need for an invitational approach to education has never been greater.

Inviting School Success begins with a definition of *invitations,* an explanation of the nature of invitations found in schools, and a description of the teacher's power to send invitations. The opening chapters describe the formal and informal, verbal and nonverbal, witting and unwitting ways in which students are powerfully "invited" or "disinvited" in their school careers. Using recent research findings regarding the importance of self-concept, these chapters present arguments that favor an invitational approach to teaching and learning.

The middle chapters describe the importance of the teacher's positive view of students and offer ways to put these views into classroom practice. Almost everyone extends invitations from time to time, but those sent by invitational teachers reflect particular beliefs about themselves, others, and the world. Their invitations are intentional, developed to high proficiency by practice and experience, and delivered with special skill. These teachers maintain respect for students and responsibility for the invitations they extend. As one student wrote, "Miss Penn invited us to like ourselves and to take pride in our work. She expected a great deal of us, and we did not let her down."

The concluding chapters focus on specific ways to invite learning. The Florida Key (Purkey, Cage, and Graves, 1973) provides a basis for exploring four ingredients of a positive self-concept as learner. The final chapter presents the concept of the invitational school. This school is based on a *family model*, characterized by warmth, cooperative spirit, and positive expectations.

I have written *Inviting School Success* so it can be useful in various courses, such as methods, curriculum, educational psychology, foundations of education, and introduction to education. Its small size and compact nature will appeal to teachers in training at both graduate and undergraduate levels and to professionals in schools of teacher education as well as those in actual daily contact with students. These include principals, supervisors, counselors, school psychologists—and all helpers who wish to improve the quality of education for all students.

These are some of the people who contributed the most to my understanding of invitations: my wife, Imogene Hedrick Purkey, who twenty-six years ago accepted my invitation to spend our lives together; my high-school teachers, Mrs. Field, Miss Penn, and Mr. Johnson, who saw things that others missed; my University of Virginia professors, Richard Beard and Virgil Ward, who invited me to grow intellectually; my friends Hal Altmann, Richard Aubry, Don Avila, Lee Bard, Charles Branch, Walter Busby, Art Combs, Sandi Damico, Mike Fagan, Cheryl Gowie, Sandi Inglis, Alan Kirby, Pam Leary, Hal Lewis, Don McFayden, John Novak, Frank Pajaras, Betty and Joel Siegel, Earl and Lynda Varnes, Mark Wasicsko, Hannelore Wass, and Harry Wong—among others who were and are the source of countless invitations . . . many thanks.

I am grateful also to Richard Coop, University of North Carolina at Chapel Hill; Frank R. Cross, Oregon State University; Jack Schmidt, University of North Carolina at Greensboro; Todd Shirley, Iowa State University; and Thomas Ringness, University of Wisconsin. Their reviews enabled me to penetrate deeply into the world of invitations.

On a personal note, my excitement and enthusiasm as I wrote this book would be difficult to overestimate. I wholeheartedly invite you to share these ideas and validate them against your own relationships with students of all ages. I hope you will find yourself agreeing with the third-grader who wrote, "I like *enventasions!*"

William Watson Purkey

Chapter One

INTRODUCTION TO INVITATIONAL EDUCATION

I now believe there is no biological, geographical, social, economic, or psychological determiner of man's condition that he cannot transcend if he is suitably invited or challenged to do so.

Sidney Jourard
Disclosing Man to Himself
(1968, p. 58)

What can educators do to create schools that encourage the realization of human potential? Our contention is that educators as well as everybody and everything involved in the educative process can—and should—*invite* school success.

Just as everyone and everything in hospitals should encourage healing, everyone and everything in schools should invite the realization of human potential. This involves the *people* (teachers, bus drivers, aides, cafeteria staff, secretaries, librarians, nurses, counselors, custodians, crossing guards, administrators), the *places* (classrooms, offices, hallways, commons, restrooms, playing fields, gymnasiums, libraries), the *policies* (rules, codes, procedures), and the *programs* (curricular or extracurricular). Everybody and everything can and should invite students to develop intellectually, socially, psychologically, and physically. We call this entire process *invitational education*. This book offers a theory of practice for its implementation.

What Is Invitational Education?

Invitational education is the application of an emerging theory of practice. The theory is incomplete, with gaps unfilled and possibilities unexplored. Although the concept is still in its infancy, we believe it offers a defensible approach to the educative process and a practical way to make school "the most inviting place in town."

Invitational education is a perceptually based, self-concept approach to the educative process and professional functioning that centers on four basic principles: (1) people are able, valuable, and responsible and should be treated accordingly; (2) teaching should be cooperative activity; (3) people possess relatively untapped potential in all areas of human development; and (4) this potential can best be realized by places, policies, and programs that are specifically designed to invite development, and by people who are personally and professionally inviting to themselves and others.

The practice of invitational education is based on an understanding of intrapersonal, interpersonal, and institutional messages intended/not intended, extended/not extended, received/not received, acted upon/not acted upon. This understanding is used to develop educational environments that are anchored in attitudes of respect, care, and civility, and that promote positive relationships and encourage human potential.

The term *invitational education* was chosen because the two words have special meaning. Our English word *invite* is probably a derivative of the Latin word *invitare,* which can mean "to offer something *beneficial* for consideration." Translated literally, *invitare* means "to summon cordially, not to shun." The word *education* comes from the Latin word *educare,* which means to "draw out" or "call forth" something potential or latent.

Literally, then, invitational education is the process by which people are cordially summoned to realize their relatively boundless potential.

What, then, is invitational education? Although our entire book expands on the question, this opening chapter provides a brief overview of its development and presents some of its basic assumptions. Various aspects of invitational education, along with practical applications, are presented as we move through this book.

The Development of Invitational Education

The development of invitational education began as an attempt to find a systematic way of describing the process of communication between teachers and students that results in learning. Despite thousands of research studies, articles, books, and reports, there is very little agreement on the nature of good teaching. This lack of agreement has been documented by Brophy and Evertson (1976) and others.

In looking at what actually happens when teaching occurs, a growing body of research points to the teacher—his or her attentiveness, expectations, encouragements, attitudes, and evaluations—as the primary focus in influencing students' perceptions of themselves as learners. There is ample research evidence that these teacher characteristics increase or decrease the probability of student learning (Braun, 1976; Brophy, 1979; Doyle, Hancock, and Kifer, 1972; Good, 1981; Mendels and Flanders, 1973; Rist, 1970; M. Smith, 1980; Turner, 1982; Wasicsko, 1977; and others).

Beyond the "hard" data, countless anecdotal self-reports describe the impact of teacher behavior on student self-concept and success in school. "After completing high school and working on the railroad for a year," a student wrote, "I decided to apply for admission to college. I went to the head of my high school English department for a recommendation. I was afraid he would look at me with skepticism, for I was a graduate of the general program. But instead, he looked at me, smiled and said: 'I was hoping that you would decide to do this.' What an invitation!"

Similar reports on the impact of the actions of significant others—the significant people in our lives—on self-concept and behavior also have been reported in professions other than teaching. The field of medicine recognizes that certain sicknesses (iatrogenic diseases) can result from the physician's witting or unwitting signals to patients to consider themselves less than healthy *(Dorland's,* 1974). (Can you imagine the impact of a medical doctor's statement to you that "your heart is not as strong as we would like it to be"?) In clinical psychology, it is believed that improved behavior results from therapy primarily because of the attitudinal qualities of the relationship, which encourage a positive, realistic self-concept in clients (Rogers, 1973, 1974). "It was not what he knew, but who he was, that seemed to help me the most," wrote one client. Moreover, Clark (1974),

Farina (1976), Rosenhan (1973), and others have demonstrated that mental hospital personnel influence patients to conform to contemporary ideas of how patients should behave. This phenomenon was dramatized in Ken Kesey's novel *One Flew over the Cuckoo's Nest* (1962). Nurse Ratched kept reminding the other hospital personnel, "This is an institution for the insane. . . . It is important to get patients adjusted to their surroundings." In the helping professions the nature of attitudes, reflected in the messages individuals send and receive, plays a profound role in determining what becomes of people.

Research on the effects of attitudes on behavior is expanding rapidly in many professional fields, and trying to keep up with it is like trying to drink water from a fire hose! Invitational education is offered in an attempt to synthesize these research findings so that educators can bring into focus the countless, and often unrecognized, processes whereby students and others in school settings learn to see themselves as responsible, capable, and valuable—or as irresponsible, incapable, and worthless. These self-perceptions, as Bloom (1980), Felice (1975), Purkey (1970), Wylie (1979), and others have documented, are basic ingredients in human behavior.

Life in and around Schools

You send strange invitations, Sir!
Beauty
Beauty and the Beast

Inviting and disinviting messages take countless forms and deal with all human interactions. Their presence has been documented by Inglis (1976), Lambeth (1980), Turner (1982), and others. People are surrounded by these messages, from formal requests to informal urgings, from verbal comments to nonverbal behaviors, from official policies and programs to unwritten traditions and agendas. Individually and collectively, these messages play a significant role in student success or failure in school.

As used here, an *inviting message* is a summary description of the content of those communications—transmitted by people, places, policies, or programs—that presents something beneficial for consideration and acceptance. At heart, an inviting message is a "doing with" rather than "doing to" process. It is an effort to establish cooperative interactions. These messages are intended to inform people that they are valuable, able, and responsible, that they have opportunities to participate meaningfully in worthwhile activities, and that they are invited to take advantage of these opportunities.

An inviting message may be as formal as a bronze pin presented at an assembly awards program, an assignment to a special project, or a note of praise sent to parents. It may also be as informal as a teacher taking special notice of a child's new shoes, as subtle as providing a cough drop for a nagging cough, or as nonverbal as a smile, nod, pat, or wink. Even several seconds of silence ("wait-time") at the right moment can be most inviting. Conversely, a disinviting message informs its recipients that they are irresponsible, incapable, and worthless and that they cannot participate in actions of any significance.

Teacher Expectancies

The subtle, but pervasive presence of inviting and disinviting messages in and around schools has been documented by the findings of classroom interaction studies. Teachers tend to exhibit more positive nonverbal behavior (smiles, nods, winks) to students considered bright than to those considered dull (Chaikin and Sigler, 1973). Teachers also teach more to, spend more time with, and request more from students they consider to be able (Baker and Crist, 1971). Furthermore, "least-efficient" learners are more likely to be ignored (Willis, 1970), to receive less attention (Rothbart, Dalfen, and Barrett, 1971), and to be given fewer opportunities to respond (Good, 1970). Based on the image of their ability and potential in the minds of teachers, certain students receive a disproportionate number of inviting messages while others are disinvited, either intentionally or unintentionally.

The influence of teacher attitudes on student achievement continues to receive considerable attention. Some studies have failed to provide evidence that teacher expectancy influences student performance (Fielder, Cohen, and Finney, 1971; Wilkins and Glock, 1973), but most research findings support the view that students are more than likely to perform as their teachers think they will (Brophy and Evertson, 1976; McDonald and Elias, 1976; Rutter, Maughan, Mortimore, Ouston, and Smith, 1979; among others). As Brophy and Good (1974) concluded from their extensive research: "When teachers had higher expectations for students, they actually produced higher achievement in those students than in students for whom they had lower expectations" (p. 80).

Perhaps the best-known study of teacher expectancy is that of Rosenthal and Jacobson (1968a, 1968b), who reported success in influencing student performance by giving teachers favorable data about selected students. Rosenthal and Jacobson's research, reported in their book *Pygmalion in the Classroom* (1968a), received criticism for its methodology, but critics have not questioned its basic assumption that teacher attitudes influence student performance. Although conclusions remain tentative, available evidence indicates that teachers do hold different expectations for various students, that these expectations influence teacher behavior, and that this behavior influences student self-perceptions and school achievement.

Brophy and Good (1974) expressed their view of teacher expectations in this statement: "Regardless of where one stands concerning Rosenthal and Jacobson's original data, work by a large number of investigators using a variety of methods over the past several years has established unequivocally that teachers' expectations can and do function as self-fulfilling prophecies, although not always or automatically" (p. 32). The subtle, indirect ways in which a prophecy is fulfilled are reflected in this college student's account of a disinviting message. "When I was in the third grade, a choral teacher said I was a good listener. Everyone laughed . . . except me. I've never uttered a musical note in public from that day to this." Another student might have taken the teacher's message humorously, but this student took it as very disinviting.

Related studies continue in the areas of teacher belief systems, teacher attentiveness, teacher enthusiasm, and teacher evaluations. On the basis of available research as well as anecdotal evidence, it is clear that teachers use both verbal and nonverbal communication systems to signal their attitudes. "My mother and I moved from rural South Carolina to upstate Michigan," a high-school girl wrote. "When I entered the Michigan school, I shyly approached my new teacher. I repeated my name when she failed to understand me the first time. 'Audrey,' the teacher asked, 'where are you from?' 'South Carolina,' I said. 'You see, my father died, and we had to move here.' 'Well, Audrey,' she responded, 'you're in the North now, and you should start speaking like a Northerner.' She didn't care what I had just said about my father." The belief systems of teachers, communicated in their inviting or disinviting messages, have a significant impact on student attitudes and behavior.

Student Attitudes

The studies mentioned so far document the presence of differential teacher expectations and treatment of students, but they do not explain the factors that prompt these beliefs and behaviors. Although many researchers have focused on teacher attitudes and actions, it is obvious that student attitudes also elicit certain expectancies and behaviors in teachers. In other words, students invite or disinvite teachers just as teachers invite or disinvite students.

That students influence teacher behavior has been documented by Bellack, Kliebard, Hyman, and Smith (1966) and Good (1980). Regardless of the presence or absence of inviting or disinviting messages from students, however, teachers have the ability and responsiblity to invite all students consistently and dependably. The teacher who excuses his or her lack of inviting messages to students by saying "When students invite me, I'll invite them" is like a governor who says "When we get better prisoners, we'll have better prisons." The teacher is the professional person in the relationship. He or she is, or should be, the primary source of inviting messages.

The power to invite, regardless of student apathy, inadequate facilties, restrictive policies, barren programs, or dispirited colleagues, lies within each professional. This power is increased or decreased by the total environment, but it is always present. We call this power *professional efficacy*.

Professional Efficacy

The professional capacity to invite or disinvite, to determine who will be invited or disinvited and how, and to establish the rules under which inviting or disinviting messages are extended rests with each educator. No matter how difficult the situation, a teacher never loses the ability to behave in a professionally inviting manner. This is an ability that educators can control and for which they can be responsible.

Recognizing, accepting, and using the ability to behave in a personally and professionally inviting manner can be a tremendous asset for educators. "Yes, I remember a most definite invitation," a student wrote. "I was at my desk, and I was twisting a ring around my finger. My teacher must have noticed, because he said, 'Cynthia, I can tell you're nervous about something. May I help?' Well, I was so impressed because I thought he could read my mind. I also thought what a marvelous person he is to be so perceptive and to really know and care how I felt inside." The inviting messages of a single teacher may not always be sufficient, but they can be significant. If nothing more, these messages probably have a cumulative effect, increasing the likelihood that other invitations will be accepted at some future time.

The Cumulative Effect of Experience

The cumulative effect of experiences is an important principle of human development. As explained by Combs, Avila, and Purkey (1978), "Life is not reversible; every experience a person has is forever. One cannot unexperience what has happened! Every experience of significant interaction has its impact upon those who were involved in it. Meaningful experiences provided by a helper may not be sufficient to produce the changes hoped for; but they are always important" (p. 31). Any message that invites people to be able, valuable, and responsible is not wasted. Each one, no matter how small or in what area, potentially can make a contribution to an individual's sense of self-esteem and his or her future development—particularly if the message is accepted and acted upon successfully.

The Importance of Consistency

Recognizing the power to send inviting messages and understanding the significance of these messages can provide educators with the confidence and strength to be consistently inviting in the face of apparent apathy, indifference, or rejection. Whether an educator's invitations are accepted or rejected depends on many factors. There are countless reasons why invitations go unaccepted that have little or nothing to do with the inviter. Behavior is determined by a lifetime of meanings that influence how individuals see themselves, others, and the world. The task of the educator, therefore, is to consistently extend appropriate invitations to learning, to note carefully how they appear in the eyes of students, and to respond accordingly with additional ones.

To be consistently inviting teachers must understand that fundamental changes in students occur slowly. Sometimes educators do not ever see the final results of their efforts. The influence of an inviting message may not be visible for weeks, months, or even years. Fortunately, invitations to see oneself in basically positive ways can be accepted and acted upon long after they are extended. One graduate student wrote: "When I was in the fifth grade, I was very sick and almost died. My teacher called our home every day. Later when I returned to school, he helped me catch up. I'll always remember his kindness, and someday I hope to write a book which says: 'Dedicated to Mr. Norman Siegal.'"

Patterns of Communication

The process of inviting the development of human potential is highly complex. Invitations are often intangible and can be so subtle and indirect that individuals are sometimes unaware of their effects. A certain pattern exists, however, in the endless variety of messages transmitted in and around schools. By bringing this pattern into focus, we can identify factors that result in students feeling invited or disinvited in school. Let us consider these in turn.

Feeling Invited

Over the past few years, more than three thousand students at various academic levels have provided examples of inviting or disinviting messages they received during their years of schooling. The great majority of students remember clearly what it was like to feel invited in school. Their illustrations fell into one of three categories: (1) valuable, (2) able, and (3) responsible. Here are some examples given by students of various ages.

Valuable

"Mr. Toppe cared enough to come to school a half hour early each morning just to help me with math."

"The teacher treated us like we were somebody. I recall the time she invited all of us to her home for a cookout."

"The first day of school my teacher said she was going to teach me how to smile . . . and she did."

"Our teacher kept us in during a recess and taught us how to sit. All the girls felt like we were being invited to be ladies."

"My first grade teacher kissed me once."

"The principal remembered my name."

"I could tell the counselor was genuinely interested in me. She listened."

Able

"Mr. Mac said I had made the most progress of anyone in the class."

"I remember my science teacher saying I was a careful researcher."

"My teacher asked me if she could take a copy of my paper to show at a teacher workshop."

"She was enthusiastic about my poetry and arranged to have it entered in a contest."

"Coach said I had natural ability."

"Mrs. Warren would write *'très bon'* on our papers when she was pleased."

"My English teacher, Mr. Maras, always said: 'Be great!'"

Responsible

"Coach asked me to take the equipment out and explain the rules."

"She didn't try to force us to work, but she made it clear that we would hurt ourselves by goofing off."

"When I decided to choose French over Spanish, I could tell that the Spanish teacher respected my decision."

"She let us do something on our own, she trusted us."

"I remember my third-grade teacher telling me how proud she was of our behavior during her absence—she said we were like sixth-graders!"

Again and again, students reported that certain teachers had a flair for inviting. They felt that their teachers were partners in learning. One student wrote: "Whenever I was in Miss Penn's English class, I could feel myself becoming more intelligent!" In light of these comments it is not surprising that students learn best when placed in the care of educators who invite them to see themselves as valuable, able, and responsible, and to behave accordingly.

Unfortunately, many students describe memories of their schooling that center on feelings of being worthless, incapable, and irresponsible.

When asked to describe the messages they received in school, these students reported feelings of being disinvited.

Feeling Disinvited

Many students reported that they felt disinvited in school because they were consistently overlooked. They said they were seldom encouraged to participate in school activities, that they rarely played on a team, belonged to a club, held an office, attended a school function, or were even called on in class. They stated that they simply did not feel a part of school and that they seldom related with faculty and staff in even the most casual way. Their teachers usually returned papers without comment except for a letter grade and rarely seemed to notice the students' absences from school. These students suffered from a "caring disability"; not enough educators cared to invite them to participate in school life.

A vivid portrait of a disinvited child is presented by Mizer (1964), who describes how schools can function to turn a child into "a zero." Mizer illustrates the tragedy of one such child, concluding her article with these words (p. 10):

> I look up and down the rows carefully each September at the
> unfamiliar faces. I look for veiled eyes or bodies scrounged
> into a seat in an alien world. "Look, kids," I say silently, "I may
> not do anything else for you this year, but not one of you is
> going to come out of here a nobody. I'll work or fight to the
> bitter end doing battle with society and the school board, but
> I won't have one of you coming out of here thinking of
> himself as a zero.

Humans need invitations the way flowers need sunshine. If students are to flourish in school they must have an environment that nurtures their potential. When they are treated with indifference, they are likely to become indifferent to themselves and to school. They begin to say to themselves, "Give up, no one cares about your small victories." This general process has been described by Willis (1970) as *systematic extinction*. What it means for the educator is that students who have learned to feel bad about themselves as learners are vulnerable to failure, just as physically weak people are susceptible to illness.

Adding to the problem of indifferent treatment, students who constantly feel disinvited may decide to seek revenge. Most students are acutely aware when some are given more opportunities and encouragement than others. As our colleague Betty Siegel remarked, "They feel there's a party going on and they haven't been invited." Those who feel disinvited remember keenly the slights they receive. And one angry student bent on destrucion can vandalize an entire school, just as one frustrated person with a rifle can redirect the course of human history.

In equally tragic shape are students who are not just ignored but who are actively dissuaded from attending school. As one middle-school student wrote, "I really don't have enough time to tell how many times I've been disinvited in school." Much of this dissuasion can be traced to formal school policy. According to recent U.S. census data, two million children miss all or a substantial portion of their school year. *The Children's Defense Fund of the Washington Research Project* (1975) concluded that these children were absent not simply by choice but because they were systematically excluded.

Since 1970 the use of suspensions as disciplinary actions in public schools has reached staggering proportions. In the 1972–73 school year, school districts enrolling over half the student population of the United States suspended one out of every twenty-four students. More striking, the suspension rate for black secondary school students was one out of eight! These figures do not include *de facto* suspensions, where students are suspended, never return, and are reported as dropouts *(Children's Defense Fund,* 1975).

Contrary to popular fears about violence in schools, the vast majority of school suspensions were for nonviolent offenses such as truancy, tardiness, pregnancy, smoking, violation of dress code, or failure to purchase required materials and equipment *(Children's Defense Fund,* 1975). Fortunately, there is growing recognition among educators and the public that students have constitutional rights to attend school and to receive an education, and that these rights cannot be denied without a formal review and due process considerations.

The problem of being educationally disenfranchised is compounded among lower socioeconomic groups, where students are sometimes more "disinvited" than disadvantaged. In his research on the self-fulfilling prophecy in ghetto education, Rist (1970) concluded that teachers inadvertently stratify students in accordance with perceived social-class membership. This tends to perpetuate a caste system that reinforces group prejudices and antagonisms in many classrooms, adding further fuel to the fires of disenfranchisement.

Labeling and Grouping

Another practice that can disinvite many children from achieving in school is that of labeling and grouping. Although some classification is essential, educators are growing more concerned about the proliferation of new syndromes. According to many experts, the negative consequences of labeling and grouping may outweigh the intended benefits of meeting the academic needs of students who require special help (Findley and Bryan, 1975; Hobbs, 1975a, 1975b). As Hobbs (1975b) warns: "Categories and labels are powerful instruments for social regulation and control, and they often are employed for obscure, covert or hurtful purposes: to de-

grade people, to deny them access to opportunity, to exclude 'undesir-
ables' whose presence in society in some way offends, disturbs familiar
customs, or demands extraordinary efforts" (p. 10). Rist (1970) has also
described this locking-in process whereby untold numbers of children are
classified in their earliest days of schooling as retarded, learning-disabled,
emotionally disturbed, hyperkinetic, brain-dysfunctioned, cognitively disadvantaged, maladjusted, or simply as slow learners. These children are
then sorted, separated, grouped, and treated differently than are "normal"
students. This differential treatment is often perpetuated year after year,
particularly when some educators pay greater attention to the label than to
the child.

A vivid example of how labels can disinvite is provided by Bogdan and
Taylor (1976). A twenty-six year old man who had been labeled mentally
retarded told the reseachers:

> The problem is getting labeled as being something. After that
> you're not really seen as a person. It's like a sty in your
> eye—it's noticeable. Like that teacher and the way she looked
> at me. In the fifth grade—in the fifth grade my classmates
> thought I was different, and my teacher *knew* I was different.
> One day she looked at me and she was on the phone in the
> room. I was there. She looked at me and knew I was
> knowledgeable about what she was saying. Her negative
> picture of me stood out like a sore thumb (p. 48.).

Institutional practices that diagnose "deviates" and bracket them in modified programs encourage both teachers and parents to expect certain
levels of performance that may doom some children to educational in-
feriority. "In our school," one student commented, "the special class is a
garbage disposal."

Research evidence on how labeling influences perceptions has been
provided by Frericks (1974), who demonstrated the effects of telling
prospective teachers that a classroom of students viewed on videotape was
a class of "low-ability" students. A control group watched the same
videotape but was told that it showed "regular students in a normal classroom." After watching the videotape, both groups of prospective teachers
completed a scale designed to measure their attitudes toward the
videotaped students. Compared to the control group, the experimental
group who had been told the students were "low-ability" viewed them as
less responsible, possessing less self-control, more prone to rudeness, and
showing less capacity to engage in an abstract level of discussion. These
findings, like those of other studies, indicate that labeling and grouping can
carry a number of penalities.

In reading, for example, some teachers tend to express negative
feelings toward children of lower-skill reading groups and tend to have

"inappropriately low expectations" for them (Brophy and Good, 1974, p. 81). One student described the stigmatizing process this way: "It's OK to be clumsy, and it's OK to be silly, but if you're both clumsy and silly, you're labeled a 'retard.'" For too many students, the school can be a high-risk neighborhood.

Evidence that labeling and grouping have the power to stigmatize students continues to accumulate. As Findley and Bryan (1975) state: "Assignment to achievement groups carries a stigma that is generally more debilitating than relatively poor achievement in heterogeneous groups" (p. 20). "When they put me in the bonehead class," one student wrote, "I wanted to walk out the door and never come back." In view of the potentially disinviting qualities of excessive labeling and rigid ability grouping, it seems tragic that these practices continue to be so widespread.

There are positive signs, however, that labeling and ability grouping are abating. Major efforts are being made to alter policies that disinvite students and contribute to the problems of low achievement. Approaches such as mainstreaming are being used to avoid the labeling and isolating of students into pejorative environments. More sensitive and discriminating ways are beginning to focus on specific problems and behaviors of individual children. Throughout the helping professions, there is a fresh appreciation for individual uniqueness and a growing awareness of the disinviting aspects of labeling and grouping.

Negative Messages

Beyond the formal school policies of suspending, expelling, labeling, tracking, and grouping, many students are disinvited by educators who, either intentionally or unintentionally, behave in ways that result in student embarrassment, frustration, and failure. "My Latin teacher did not like females, particularly 'socially oriented' ones," a high-school girl wrote. "And I met both requirements. I was in a room with my best friends, which included males and females. The teacher would pick me out and have me go to the board and write something in Latin. Of course, when I missed something, which was often, the entire class got a lecture on studying more and socializing less. But I had to stand in front of the class by myself the entire time while the lecture on the evils of 'socializing' was being presented. I was usually so embarrassed I would end up crying in the bathroom where no one could see me."

Canfield and Wells (1976) use the term *killer statements* to describe the means by which a student's feelings, thoughts, and creativity are "killed off" by another person's negative comments, physical gestures, or other behaviors. These actions may be little more than a teacher's suddenly stiffened spine when a child of another race touches his or her shoulder— or as elusive as the failure to call on or even look at certain children.

A child's feelings of being disinvited are described by Dick Gregory in his autobiography *Nigger* (1964): "The teacher thought I was a troublemaker. All she saw from the front of the room was a little black boy who squirmed in his idiot's seat and made noises and poked the kids around him. I guess she couldn't see a kid who made noises because he wanted someone to know he was there" (p. 30). People have profound influence on each other; whether intentional or unintentional, disinviting messages can have long-lasting effects.

Students who reported that they felt disinvited in school described experiences that could be divided into three categories of self-perception: (1) worthless, (2) unable, and (3) irresponsible. Here are some examples.

Worthless

"On the first day of school, the teacher came in and said he wasn't supposed to teach this basic class, but that he was stuck with us."

"My name is Bill Dill, but the teacher always called me 'Dill Pickle' and laughed."

"One teacher told me I just wanted to cause trouble all the time."

"The teacher said 'That's crazy! What's the matter with you?' His negative attitude toward me stood out like a bump on your nose."

"I transferred to a new school after it had started. When I appeared at the teacher's doorway, she said 'Oh, no, not another one!'"

"My teacher told me I was the worst kid she ever taught."

Unable

"They put me in the dummy class, and it had *Special Education* painted right on the door."

"The teacher said to me in front of the whole class: 'I really don't think you're that stupid.'"

"The principal showed me to the visitor as an example of a 'slow child' who could dress nice."

"When the principal hit me, he said it was the only language I understood."

"They kept telling me I got to learn to keep my mouth shut and stay in my seat."

"I was asked if I had enough sense to follow simple directions."

Irresponsible

"The teacher said I didn't want to learn, that I just wanted to cause trouble."

"She said I was worse than my brother, and I don't even have a brother."

"Because I failed to bring my homework, the counselor asked me why I bothered coming to school."

"She told the class we were discipline problems and were not to be trusted."

"The teacher put me out in the hall for everyone to laugh at."

"The coach told me he couldn't count on me for anything important."

Of course, negative experiences may spur someone to future success, but this is likely to be true only of students who do not easily accept rejection and failure. Students who fight back against disinviting experiences do so only because they have a past history of invitations received, accepted, and successfully acted upon. They have built up a partial immunity to failure. Students who readily accept disinviting messages about themselves and their abilities are usually those who have been infected with failure early in life. As one student wrote: "Hell, how can I feel good about myself when I'm stuck in the dummy class year after year?"

The picture drawn from countless descriptions is that students live in a world of attitudes, expectancies, and evaluations. The full impact of this world has yet to be determined, but it seems clear that student success or failure is related to the ways in which students perceive themselves and their environments—and that these perceptions are influenced by the prevailing nature of the messages they receive in school.

Importance of the Inviting Approach

Everything the teacher does, as well as the manner in which he does it, incites the child to respond in some way or another and each response tends to set the child's attitude in some way or another.
John Dewey
How We Think
(1933, p. 59)

Current research evidence is scarce, but it can be hypothesized that individuals have a basic need to be noticed, and noticed favorably, by others. As William James (1890) commented long ago: "No more fiendish punishment could be devised, were such a thing possible, than that one should be turned loose in society and remain absolutely unnoticed by all the members thereof" (p. 179). This basic need for affirmation has also been described by Martin Buber: "Man wishes to be confirmed in his being by man, and wishes to have a presence in the being of the other. . . . secretly and bashfully he watches for a Yes which allows him to be and which can come only from one human person to another. It is from one person to another that the heavenly bread of self-being is passed" (1965, p. 71). Thus, we create one another.

Following Buber's thinking, it appears that no one is self-made. Each day students are influenced by the way the school bus driver greets them as they step on the bus, by the policies established by the school board, by the way the food is prepared and served in the cafeteria. They are also influenced by the ways the physical environment is maintained, by the way classes are conducted, and by the nature and availability of programs. Everything in the school counts, either positively or negatively.

Of all the things that count, nothing is as important as the people in the process. Teaching machines, microcomputers, programmed materials, and other technological advances may have an important place in education, but they cannot substitute for human relationships. As Jourard (1968) indicated, teaching is a way of being with people. This "being-with" process has a great impact on students' ideas about themselves and their abilities.

Even more than "being with," invitational education suggests a bidding to be somewhere, to see people not only as they are but also as they might become, to look ahead to tomorrow's joy and fulfillment. Most educators who have been in schools awhile understand the importance of having a positive vision of the future. This was described by an elementary school teacher who wrote: "Recently in my second-grade class I had each child express what he or she would like to be as an adult. After listening to each child, I said: 'Everybody look up at your star in the sky and reach for it!' Every child in the room started reaching as high as possible. The amazing thing is that they all wanted to learn something each day just so I can say to them: 'Reach up and see if you're a little bit closer to your star.'" Each human watches closely for clues in the behavior of others. A teacher's words, winks, smiles, nods, or touches can be marvelously reassuring to a child struggling with a difficult spelling word, a complex math problem, a threatening oral report, or an effort to reach a star. Successful teachers realize that humans are in the process of being created. They use this realization to develop appropriate and caring patterns of communication.

Levels of Functioning

Teacher: Would you like me to refer to you as Negro or black?
Student: I think I would like to be referred to as Joanne.

Earlier the idea was presented that each professional has the ability and responsibility to function in a professionally inviting manner. However, it is possible for a message to be *unintentionally* inviting, or disinviting, for what is attractive or repellent remains in the eyes of the beholder. There is no guarantee that the most well-intentioned actions will be viewed positively by others.

There are probably numerous classification systems available for categorizing messages. The classification system that fits the approach presented in this book involves the following four categories: *Level One:* intentionally disinviting; *Level Two:* unintentionally disinviting; *Level Three:* unintentionally inviting; and *Level Four:* intentionally inviting. Let us consider these four levels more closely.

Level One: Intentionally Disinviting

It is painful to acknowledge that there are some messages that are meant to be disinviting. Comments such as "You must give up those shiftless habits" or "You never use your head" fit into this level. Professionals functioning at the intentionally disinviting level are aware of the disabling, demeaning, and devaluing potential of their behavior. Exactly why some few people choose to function at this bottom level and serve as a damaging presence is unclear. Regardless of the reasons—whether because of racial prejudice, unrequited love, personal inadequacy, or negative self-image—they might benefit from professional help. If they are unable or unwilling to accept help, it is the responsibility of fellow professionals, caringly but firmly, to remove them from daily contact with students. From an invitational education viewpoint, there is no justification for *Level One* behavior on the part of professionals.

Fortunately, relatively few educators function at *Level One* for any extended period of time. Intentionally disinviting messages are usually communicated in fits of anger or frustration. Here is an extreme example provided by a student:

> When I was in kindergarten, Mrs. Hall made me sit beside Ilmar. No one wanted to sit next to him because he smelled bad and always had a runny nose. One day he bit me on the arm. I told Mrs. Hall and she said if he did it again he would have to move. So JoLynn (my friend) said she would bite my arm (teeth marks for proof) and I could tell Mrs. Hall. When I showed Mrs. Hall my arm she became furious. She asked me if I wanted to bite Ilmar back. Of course I didn't, so she bit him on the arm.

A major problem with *Level One* behavior is that these intentionally disinviting actions tend to be justified by some individuals as being "good for students." From our understanding of the effects of such behavior, this is certainly not the case. Moreover, we can think of no circumstances in which a professional can justify intentionally disinviting behavior.

Another form of intentionally disinviting behavior is exhibited by the person who sends mixed, but predominantly disinviting messages. People who behave this way mean to be disinviting, but may alter their behavior when confronted. For example, in the movie *On Golden Pond,* Norman (Henry Fonda) often exhibited disinviting behaviors, but when confronted by his young friend or daughter he was willing to change. Sometimes such confrontation can be beneficial to those involved. If intentionally disinviting messages in schools go unchallenged, then schools may move away from their primary function—to invite human potential.

Level Two: Unintentionally Disinviting

A much larger problem in schools stems from the people, places, policies, and programs that are unintentionally disinviting. Educators who operate at *Level Two* are typically well meaning, but their behavior is often seen by others as chauvinistic, condescending, or simply thoughtless. Comments such as "What Earl is trying to say" and "It's easy, anyone can do it" typify this level. Professionals who function at *Level Two* spend a lot of time wondering "What did I do wrong?" "Why aren't my students learning more?" "Why is everyone so upset with me?"

Teaching that is unintentionally disinviting is often characterized by boredom, busywork, and insensitivity to feelings. Examples of such insensitivity appear again and again in student accounts of being disinvited: "I feel insulted when faculty sponsors always ask a female to take minutes," wrote one girl. Another student described how she was disinvited by a teacher who said: "You're invited to try out for the part . . . if you really want to." A third student complained that the teacher always used the term "broken home" when he could just as easily have said "single-parent family." Teacher behavior perceived by students as sexist, racist, patronizing, or thoughtless is likely to be interpreted as disinviting despite the teacher's good intention.

Level Three: Unintentionally Inviting

Educators functioning at *Level Three* seem to have stumbled into particular ways of functioning that are usually effective, but they have a difficult time explaining why. As good as they often are, they usually lack a consistent stance from which to operate. Many so-called natural-born teachers, those who may never have thought much about what they are doing but who are highly effective in the classroom, are successful because they are functioning at *Level Three*. They typically behave in ways that result in student feelings of being invited, although they are largely unaware of the dynamics involved.

Professionals who function at *Level Three* are like the early "barnstorming" airplane pilots. These pioneer pilots didn't know a lot about aerodynamics, weather patterns, or navigation. As long as they stayed close to the ground and the weather was clear, so they could follow the highways and railroad tracks, they did fine. However, when the weather turned ugly or night fell, they became disoriented and got lost. In difficult situations they lacked consistency in direction.

The problem of functioning at the unintentionally inviting level is that the educator can become disoriented and unable to identify the reasons for his or her successes or failures. If whatever "it" is should stop working, the teacher does not know how to start it up again, or what changes to make in his or her behavior. In other words, the teacher lacks a consistent stance—a dependable position from which to operate. A colleague of ours, Charles Branch, once remarked that there are times he would rather work with people who are functioning at *Level One* than those who are at *Level Three*. At least with *Level One* you know where you stand. The need for consistency and dependability in professional relationship brings us to *Level Four*.

Level Four: Intentionally Inviting

From the point of view presented in this book, educators should strive to be intentionally inviting. To do so requires understanding the reasons for, and the results of, one's behavior. It also requires having the desire to function in a dependably inviting manner. But even at this top level there are those who are more successful than others in their actions. Let's look at possible reasons for degrees of success within the broad category of *Level Four*.

Educators who are seeking to be intentionally inviting, but who are uncertain about the process, are going through a transition period. They begin to understand the processes involved and make a conscious effort to be inviting. However, when they face difficult situations they may resort to lower and perhaps more familiar levels of functioning. Students generally feel good about these beginning *Level Four* teachers, but may have a vague feeling that these teachers are not too dependable and can't be counted on in tough situations. With experience and practice, teachers are likely to move successfully through this transition period. Educators who are dependable in their actions consistently face diverse and difficult situations with a particular stance, which is explained in detail in Chapter 3. The importance of consistency and dependability is illustrated in the following:

Stubborn Teacher

My teacher is so stubborn! She is told that I am unmotivated.
    But she invites me anyway.
She is told that I don't want to learn.
    She invites me anyway.
She is told that I don't have the ability.
    She invites me anyway.

> She is told I just want to cause trouble.
>   She invites me anyway.
> She invites me again, and again, and again.
>   She fills my world with invitations.
> One day, I'll take the greatest risk of my life.
>   I'll accept one, and see what happens.

When educators functioning at *Level Four* perceive, choose, and act with consistency and sensitivity, they are likely to become *artfully inviting,* a term first used by our colleague Tim Gerber. At this point they have integrated *Level Four* behaviors into what appears to be an effortless activity, but what is actually the product of serious and sustained effort. The process is similar to what someone who has worked to become fluent enough in a language to think and create in it has gone through. Artfully inviting educators think in a special language of "doing with" rather than "doing to." They have developed the ability to approach even the most difficult situation in a professionally inviting manner. When educators who are functioning at this advanced level face problems, they are able to rely on their understanding of invitational education to develop solutions. Educators functioning at *Level Four* are like modern jet pilots. Thanks to their knowledge, they can "fly on instruments" if need be—around or over dangerous weather fronts. In the final analysis, it is this ability to chart and maintain a dependable "flight pattern" that makes the difference between success or failure as a teacher.

Recognition of the ability to be intentionally inviting and the artful use of this ability can be tremendous assets. By understanding the four levels of functioning, by seeking to function at the top level, and by improving abilities within this highest level, educators can be powerful forces in inviting school success.

Summary

This opening chapter has introduced the concept of invitational education and has explained how it serves as a vehicle for understanding the influence of people, places, policies, and programs on student success or failure. We have seen in Chapter 1 that some students are invited to learn, some are overlooked, and some are told to stay away. Evidence was presented to show that individuals respond best when they share the company of educators who believe them to be valuable, capable, and responsible, and who intentionally invite them to share in these beliefs.

Chapter 2 offers a detailed look at the foundations of invitational education.

Chapter Two

FOUNDATIONS OF INVITATIONAL EDUCATION

Human behavior is always a product of how people see themselves and the situations in which they are involved. Although this fact seems obvious, the failure of people everywhere to comprehend it is responsible for much of human misunderstanding, maladjustment, conflict and loneliness. Our perceptions of ourselves and the world are so real to us that we seldom pause to doubt them.

A. W. Combs, D. Avila, and W. W. Purkey
Helping Relationships, *Second Edition*
(1978, p. 15)

Any approach to education is based on certain assumptions about what people are and what they might become. This chapter considers two cornerstones on which the assumptions of invitational education are based: the perceptual tradition and the self-concept theory.

The Perceptual Tradition

Invitational education has its roots in the perceptual approach to understanding human behavior. Rather than viewing people as objects to be stimulated, shaped, modified, reinforced, and conditioned, or as captives of unconscious urges or unfulfilled desires, the perceptual tradition views people as they see themselves, others, and the world. It takes as its starting point the notion that each person is a conscious agent: he or she experiences, interprets, constructs, decides, acts, and is ultimately responsible for his or her actions.

Historically, there have been many contributions to the perceptual approach. The list is long and includes William James's description of consciousness (1890), George Herbert Mead's perspective on the social nature of perception (1934), Prescot Lecky's notion of the consistent nature of perceptions (1945), George Kelly's development of personal constructs as the basis of perceptions (1955), and Gordon Allport's (1937, 1943, 1955, 1961) and Carl Rogers's (1947, 1951, 1959, 1965, 1969, 1974, 1980) career-long emphases on people as perceptive, purposeful, and capable of taking responsibility for their present lives and future aspirations.

More recent contributions have included Sidney Jourard's use of the concept of self-disclosure (1967, 1968, 1971), William Powers's connection of perception and systems theory (1973), Martin Seligman's explanation of learned helplessness (1975; Garber and Seligman, 1980), and Robert Kegan's exploration of the evolving nature of meaning-making and perception (1982). In addition, educational research has taken seriously this turning to the perspective of the person through the growing use and refinement of qualitative research methods to investigate perceptions (Bogdan and Biklen, 1982). It appears that the perceptual approach will have an increasingly important role in understanding human behavior.

Invitational education builds on the perceptual tradition and places special emphasis on the Snygg-Combs theory of perception. This theory was first presented in systematic form in *Individual Behavior: A New Frame of Reference for Psychology* by Donald Snygg and Arthur Combs in 1949. It has been revised twice (Combs and Snygg, 1959; Combs, Richards, and Richards, 1976) and applied to teacher education (Combs, 1982; Combs, Blume, Newman, and Wass, 1974) and to the helping professions in general (Combs et al., 1978). The basic contention of this perceptual theory is that people behave according to how they see themselves and the situations in which they are involved (Combs et al., 1978, p. 15). Because of this emphasis on understanding and working with people as they see themselves and the world, perceptual theory is a type of "practitioner's" psychology (Combs et al., 1978, p. 109). This approach seems well suited for use in many professional settings, including teaching, administering, counseling, nursing, ministering, and related human service fields.

Three basic assumptions of this practitioner's psychology follow, along with examples of how they serve as bases of invitational education.

Behavior Is Based on Perceptions

The perceptual approach seeks to answer the question of why we do the things we do by postulating that "all behavior, without exception, is completely determined by, and pertinent to, the phenomenal field of the behaving organism" (Snygg and Combs, 1949, p. 15). In other words, each of us behaves according to how the world appears at the moment of behaving. From this vantage point there is no such thing as illogical behavior—every person is behaving in the way that makes the most sense to her or him at that particular instant. What may seem illogical from an external point of view is only an inadequate understanding of what the world looks like from the internal viewpoint of the behaving person. Perhaps a personal example can clarify this. A few years ago one of the authors of this book was trying to learn to hang glide. He had soloed an airplane and knew the basic rule of aerodynamics: "Thou shalt always maintain thy airspeed or thou shalt smite the ground." However, when he was taking his first "easy" flight in a hang glider that was not designed to take him more than five feet off the ground, he got caught by an updraft and was suddenly thirty-five feet high. At that moment, rather than leveling off, he closed his eyes and pushed the frame of the kite away from his body and promptly climbed up to sixty feet! Through a series of fortunate events he was able to land without being killed.

Why did he close his eyes and push the frame forward when he knew the consequences of such an action? There are various explanations for his behavior, each with its defenders. A behaviorist might conclude that he had been insufficiently reinforced in the proper way of leveling the frame and thus had not been properly conditioned to emit the correct response. A Freudian might hypothesize that perhaps he had an unconsious death wish and that his behavior was a mainfestation of this basic impulse. A perceptualist, by comparison, would try to "read behavior backwards," to discover what the world looked like to the student pilot the moment he closed his eyes and pushed the frame forward. In looking back at the incident, it seems that the person was totally surprised to be up so high so soon. At that moment he could think of nothing else but to do the safest thing he could—to close his eyes and get the frame as far away from himself as fast as possible. At that moment his reasoning was, "If I can't see the ground, it can't hurt me." Later, such thinking seemed absurd. However, at the instant of behaving, closing his eyes and pushing away the frame made the most sense.

From the perceptual point of view the fundamental unit of analysis is the way a single experiencing human being views oneself, others, and the world at a particular moment in time. As used here, *perception* refers to the differentiations a person is able to make in his or her personal world of experience. Threat narrows perception and reduces differentiations. In the hang glider example, the threatened person had a severely restricted perceptual field called "tunnel vision" (Combs et al., 1978). Because of threat and his restricted perceptual field he was able to make only limited differentiations. Thus, the perceptual tradition holds that to understand human behavior it is essential to understand how things appear from the vantage point of the active perceiver at the moment of behaving.

In addition to considering things from an internal viewpoint, the perceptual tradition holds that there is much more to the world than what is presently perceived. Thus, each person's perceptual field is capable of infinite enrichment. The ideas that we can enhance our perceptions and that our perceptual fields are capable of almost infinite expansion serve as major reasons for invitational education. Without such a belief in human potential, invitational education would be empty. With such a belief, there is something to reach for: a coming together for creative, worthwhile purposes. Recognizing that behavior is grounded in perceptions leads us to a second major grounding point of invitational education: that perceptions are learned.

Perceptions Are Learned

No one reading these words was born with the perceptions he or she presently possesses. Perceptions change over time. Through myriad encounters with the world, particularly those with significant others, people develop certain fundamental perceptions that serve as organizing filters for making sense of the world. Without such a filtering system each person would be relentlessly bombarded by unrelated stimuli, creating an infinitely chaotic existence. Without an organized "in here," there could be no organized "out there."

Our fundamental perceptions serve as our "frame of reference for judgment" (Combs et al., 1976, p. 109). Although we exist in the present, our perceptions influence the memories we use to anticipate the future. Thus, any change in our present perceptions alters our view of both the past and the future.

Invitational education is based on an understanding of and respect for people's perceptual worlds. These perceptual worlds are not to be taken lightly, for they provide the basis for behavior. How sensitive we are to how people perceive themselves, others, and the world affects the messages we choose to extend and accept. Fortunately, our sensitivity to the perceptual worlds of ourselves and others can be enhanced through reflection—which brings us to a third grounding point of invitational education.

Perceptions Can Be Reflected Upon

There is absolutely no inevitability as long as there is willingness to contemplate what is happening.
Marshall McLuhan and Quinton Fiore
The Medium Is the Massage
(1967, p. 25)

We not only perceive the world in the present, we can also reflect on our past experiences. According to John Dewey (1916), reconstruction of experience is the basis for education. This reflective process enables us to understand how our perceptions develop and where they are taking us. As Chamberlin (1981) indicated, our reflections upon the past influence our "preflections" of the future—reinterpreting past experience enables us to project new futures. Reflective thinking helps each of us to understand better what we have perceived in the past, what we are now perceiving, and what we might perceive in the future. This reflective process can create new and exciting possibilities for the realization of human potential.

The ability to examine one's perceptions is essential to invitational education. Being aware of past and present perceptions and being able and willing to go beyond them permit the development of a deeper level of understanding of self, others, and the world. As our colleague Bill Stafford noted, invitational education is more than "I feel"; it is also "I think," "I know," I reflect," "I imagine."

So far we have emphasized that people behave according to how they perceive themselves, others, and the world, that these perceptions are learned, and that they can be reflected upon. It is now time to turn our attention to what is probably the most important perception of all: self-perception.

Self-Concept Theory

You see, really and truly, apart from the things anyone can pick up (the dressing and the proper way of speaking, and so on), the difference between a lady and a flower girl is not how she behaves, but how she's treated. I shall always be a flower girl to Professor Higgins, because he treats me as a flower girl, and always will; but I know I can be a lady to you, because you always treat me as a lady, and always will.
Eliza Doolittle to Colonel Pickering
George Bernard Shaw, Pygmalion
(1940, p. 80)

Of all the perceptions we learn, none seems to affect our search for personal significance and identity more than our self-perception—our view of who we are and how we fit into the world.

Some theorists (Combs et al., 1978; Rogers, 1947, 1951, 1967; Snygg and Combs, 1949) have postulated that the maintenance, protection, and enhancement of the perceived self (one's own personal existence as viewed by oneself) is the basic motive behind all human behavior. Use of this basic assumption, organized into what is generally known as self-concept theory, can clarify and integrate seemingly unrelated aspects of life in classrooms. For example, students who have learned to see themselves as troublemakers may respond by being discipline problems, just as students who have learned to view themselves as scholars may spend many hours in libraries. The dynamics are the same, even if the resulting behaviors are quite different. An understanding of self-concept and its relation to invitational education is advantageous for educators who wish to function in a professionally inviting manner.

Over the past two decades self-concept has become a central part of many human personality theories and the basis for numerous programs in education. Led by the early pathfinding research and writings of Lecky (1945), Raimy (1948), Rogers (1951, 1967), Combs and Snygg (1959), Patterson (1961), Wylie (1961, 1974, 1979), Diggory (1966), Coopersmith (1967), Fitts and Hamner (1969), and many others, investigators have gathered a large body of empirical data on self-concept. The emerging literature is so vast that this chapter can examine in turn only three aspects of self-concept that relate most directly to invitational education: (1) self-concept development, (2) self-concept as guidance system, and (3) the significance of positive self-regard.

Self-Concept Development

I always wanted a red balloon,
It only cost a dime,
But Ma said it was risky
They broke so quickly,
And besides, she didn't have time.
And even if she did, she didn't
Think they were worth a dime.
We lived on a farm, and I only went
To one circus and fair,
And all the balloons I ever saw
Were there.
There were yellow ones and blue ones,
But the kind I like the best
Were red, and I don't see why
She couldn't have stopped and said
That maybe, I could have one . . .
But she didn't.
I suppose that now

You can buy them anywhere
And that they still sell red ones
At circuses and fairs.
I got a little money saved;
Plenty of balloons . . . but somehow
There's something died inside of me,
And I don't want one . . . now.

Jill Spargur
"Tragedy"

It appears that no one is born with a self-concept. The development and structure of self-awareness is a lifelong research project, and the ever-widening experiences of the developing person constantly modify the self-concept. By experiencing the world through inviting and disinviting interactions with significant others, as well as through similar interactions with oneself, the developing person organizes a theory of personal existence. Epstein (1973) has presented a detailed description of this process. Each person learns early to identify oneself both with categories (female, black, southerner, Canadian, Methodist, Virginian) and with attributes (good, bad, strong, weak, valuable, worthless, responsible, irresponsible, able, unable). Gradually, each individual forges a self-concept, complete with a complex hierarchy of attributes and categories. This developmental aspect of self-concept has been described in detail by numerous researchers, including Bachman and O'Malley (1977), Felker (1974), Gergen (1971), Hansen and Maynard (1973), Kegan (1982), Purkey (1970), Rosenberg (1979), and Wyne, White, and Coop (1974).

The ingredients of self-concept are primarily social, obtained through countless interactions with persons, places, policies, and programs. For example, one child announced at the dinner table that she was an honest person. When asked how she knew she was honest, she replied, "Because my teacher asked me to help her grade papers!" Children learn to see themselves as honest just as they learn to view themselves as dishonest. Each of us attributes meaning to the acts of others, and we seek to understand ourselves by studying how others relate to us. The self-concepts of students are heavily influenced by those who treat them as able, valuable, and responsible—as well as by those who treat them as unable, worthless, and irresponsible. At some level of awareness each of us is always asking a very basic question: "Who do you say I am?" The answer to this question influences how we behave and what we become.

Research on the development of self-concept supports the notion that self-evaluations are basically the products of what we think the significant people in our lives perceive us to be (Kelley, 1973; Purkey, 1970; Rosenberg, 1979; Sunby, 1971; Webster and Sobieszek, 1974). Findings indicate that, beginning early in life, infants receive countless cues as to their value in the eyes of significant others. Adults communicate these cues to the infant through their postures, facial expressions, gestures, eye contact, and other body movements as well as through their vocalizations.

Words, as Hinde (1972) demonstrated, are always accompanied by gestures that elucidate, emphasize, enhance, or even contradict the spoken word. The father who says to his small child "Of course I love you" while his eyes never leave the television set, and the teacher who speaks of her high regard for students, but shivers inside at their touch, contradict their words with their behavior. What we do speaks much louder than what we say. This is particularly true in schools, where inviting or disinviting messages can be recognized in every activity.

Next to the home, schools probably exert the single greatest influence on how students see themselves and their abilities. According to Patterson, "The concepts which the teacher has of the children become the concepts which the children come to have of themselves" (1973, p. 125). Most public-school students spend over a thousand hours per year in school. Their experiences there play a major role in determining what they think of themselves and their abilities.

One student described a school experience this way: "When I was in the fifth grade, we had a variety show every Friday afternoon. One Friday I sang a song. My teacher loved the song because her husband was in the military and far away. The song was about 'Sending myself to my loved one in a letter.' I have always tried to please my teachers, but never have I pleased anyone so much! She embraced me, both physically and psychologically, and invited me to sing before the PTA. I've been singing ever since!"

Of all the contemporary models of teaching, none depends more on the personal and professional qualities of the teacher than does invitational education. Classroom teachers, as Bugelski (1971) stressed, are stimulus objects, attractive or repellent in their own right. By their very presence they have a subtle but profound impact on students' self-concepts. The task of the teacher, therefore, is to behave in ways that encourage positive perceptions in students regarding themselves and their abilities.

As a further illustration of how a single teacher can influence a student's self-regard, one student wrote the following: "I'll never forget my seventh-grade teacher. At that time I was overweight and wore braces on my teeth. Our teacher asked us to turn in a paper of different types of sentences. To demonstrate an exaggeration, I wrote: 'I am the most beautiful girl in the world.' The teacher wrote back: 'This is an exaggeration?' He'll never know how good he made me feel."

From the moment students first make contact with school, the inviting or disinviting actions of school personnel—coupled with the physical environments, the official policies, and the instructional programs—dominate their education. Students able to meet the academic expectations of schools are likely to develop positive attitudes toward themselves as learners, and those who fail are likely to develop negative feelings. There seems to be little question that the school plays a significant role in influencing the course of development in students.

Unfortunately, a significant decrease in both self-regard and attitudes toward school apparently occurs with advances in age and grade level (Landry and Edeburn, 1974; Stanwyck and Felker, 1974). In a 1975–76 study of elementary school children and their feelings about school, the Pennsylvania Department of Education reported dramatic shifts from "happy" feelings in kindergarten to "sad" feelings by grade six. Even more significantly, 64 percent of kindergarten children expressed happy feelings about schoolwork, but by grade six, the figure had slipped to only 13 percent (Cormany, 1975). The following exemplifies how the slippage might occur: "I hate poetry," one student explained. "I remember when we misbehaved we had to stay after school and memorize a poem. I never developed anything but a bitter taste for poetry." This gradual erosion of enthusiasm for learning provides a compelling argument for more inviting schools.

Self-Concept as Guidance System

Dear, dear! How queer everything is today! And yesterday things went on just as usual. I wonder if I've been changed in the night? Let me think: Was I the same when I got up this morning? I almost think I can remember feeling a little different. But if I'm not the same, the next question is "Who in the World am I?" Ah, that's the puzzle!
Alice
Lewis Carroll
Alice in Wonderland
(1971, pp. 15–16)

A self-concept is a complex, continuously active system of subjective beliefs about personal existence. It serves to guide behavior and to enable each individual to assume particular roles in life. Rather than initiating activity, self-concept serves as a perceptual filter and guides the direction of behavior. A student's self-concept, as Spears and Deese (1973) indicated, does not *cause* the student to misbehave in the classroom. A better explanation is that the disruptive student has learned to see himself or herself as a troublemaker and behaves accordingly. In other words, self-concept serves as the reference point or anchoring perception for behavior. Shavelson, Hubner, and Stanton (1976) refer to self-concept as a "moderator variable." In practical classroom situations, students who have learned to see themselves as "schlemiels" are likely to exhibit "schlemiel" behavior.

Zimmerman and Allebrand (1965) have provided research evidence regarding the guidance function of self-concept. They demonstrated that poor readers lack a sense of personal worth and adequacy to the point where they actively avoid achievement. For poor readers, to study hard and still fail provides unbearable proof of their inadequacy. To avoid such proof and thus suffer less pain, many students deliberately choose not to try. Their defense against failure is secretly to accept themselves as failures! It is better, from the students' viewpoint, not to try than to try and be embarrassed or humiliated for trying. Glock (1972) stated the situation succinctly: "A negative self-image is its own best defender" (p. 406). To understand why this is so, it is important to recognize that from the student's perceptual vantage point any amount of anxiety, no matter how great, seems preferable to other available avenues of behavior.

Each person acts in accordance with the ways he or she has learned to see oneself. From a lifetime of studying his or her own actions and those of significant others in interaction with the self, each individual acquires expectations about what things "fit" in his or her personal world. For example, if a new experience is consistent with past experiences already incorporated into the self-concept system, the person easily accepts and assimilates the new experience. However, if the new experience is in opposition with those already incorporated, the person will probably reject it. Jersild (1952) explained it this way: "A person accepts and incorporates that which is congenial to the self-system already established, but he seeks to reject or avoid experiences or meanings of experiences which are uncongenial" (p. 14). Furthermore, actions taken that are incompatible with the self-image are likely to result in psychological discomfort and anxiety. The result is that everything a person experiences is filtered through, and mediated by, whatever self-concept is already present within the individual. This screening process insures some consistency within the human personality.

The tendency toward internal consistency appears to be a necessary feature of human personality. It provides the individual's entire being with internal balance, a sense of direction, and a feeling of stability. If individuals adopted new beliefs about themselves rapidly, or if their behaviors were capricious, no integrity would exist in the individual personality and human progress would be difficult to imagine. (Few people would risk flying if they thought the pilot might suddenly turn into Daffy Duck!) Fortunately, most people are remarkably consistent in their self-concepts.

Educators who do not recognize the conservative nature of self-concept are likely to expect quick or miraculous changes in others—such as the teacher who commented, "I'm not going to send another student to the counseling office. I sent a student yesterday. Today he's back and he hasn't changed a bit!" Self-perceptions do change, but not immediately or automatically.

One of the probable reasons for the apparent failure of many school programs designed to enhance, build, or modify students' perceptions of themselves is the tendency to overlook the conservative nature of self-concept. Whether a student's self-perception is psychologically healthy or unhealthy, educationally productive or counterproductive, the student will cling to it the way a drowning person clings to a straw. In fact, students who have learned to see themselves as stupid will experience considerable anxiety over their own successful performance. Several studies (Aronson and Carlsmith, 1962; Curtis, Zanna, and Campbell, 1975; Haan, 1963; Mettee, 1971) have indicated that students who have learned to expect failure are even likely to sabotage their own efforts when they meet unexpected success. As Jersild (1952) concluded, students are active in maintaining their self-pictures "even if by misfortune the picture is a false and unhealthy one" (p. 14).

One additional point relates to the consistency of self-concept: being correct in one's assumptions about oneself has reward value, even if the assumption is negative. A student may take a certain pleasure in thinking, "See, just as I thought, I knew nobody in this lousy school cares whether I live or die!" Being right, even about negative feelings toward oneself, can be satisfying. This is one reason why one-shot attempts, quick-fix efforts, or programs that lack consistency and dependability in direction are often unsuccessful and may even incur student resistance or anger.

Although educators should be aware that self-concepts tend toward consistency, they should also remember that changes in self-concepts are possible. New ideas filter into the self-concept throughout life while some old ideas fade away. This continuous process creates flexibility in human personality and allows for psychological development. The hypothetical reason for the assimilation of new ideas and the expulsion of old ones is that each person has a basic need to maintain, protect, and enhance the self-concept—to obtain positive self-regard as well as positive regard from others. This basic human characteristic is a tremendous given for the classroom teacher. Rather than struggling to motivate students, the teacher may assume that they are *always* motivated. Thus, the teacher can concentrate his or her energies toward influencing the direction this motivation will take. The student's motor is already running. The function of education is to place the signs, build the roads, direct the traffic, and teach good driving—but not to *drive* the car.

Let us briefly consider the nature of motivation. From a self-concept point of view (Avila and Purkey, 1966; Combs and Snygg, 1959), there is only one kind of motivation—an internal and continuous incentive that every individual has at all times, in all places, during any activity. As Combs (1962) explained: "People are always motivated; in fact, they are never unmotivated. They may not be motivated to do what we would prefer they do, but it can never be truly said that they are unmotivated" (p. 85). This view of motivation should be tremendously reassuring to teachers, for it assumes motivation is a force that comes from within the student. Rather than spending energy in trying to motivate students, teachers can use their talents to invite students to explore the world of knowledge. These invitations to learning are most likely to be accepted and acted upon when students see them as contributing to their own positive self-regard.

Significance of Positive Self-Regard

*A person who doubts himself is like a man who would enlist in the
ranks of his enemies and bear arms against himself. He makes his failure certain by himself being the first person to be convinced of it.*
Alexandre Dumas
The Three Musketeers
(1844/1962)

It seems self-evident that for students to learn in school, they require
sufficient confidence in themselves and their abilities to make some effort
to succeed. Self-regard and efforts to control one's destiny correlate highly.
As Szasz (1976) explained, "The more self-esteem a person has, the greater,
as a rule, is his desire, and his ability, to control himself" (p. 57). Without
self-confidence, students easily succumb to apathy, dependency, and loss of
self-control. The classroom result is that some students will expect the
worst in every situation and will be constantly afraid of doing the wrong
thing or saying the wrong word. Too often, the real problem of negative
self-esteem is hidden beneath such labels as *unmotivated, undisciplined,*
or *uninterested.*

The importance of positive self-regard has been documented by
Coopersmith's study of the antecedents of self-esteem among children.
Coopersmith (1967) reported: "There are pervasive and significant differences in the experiential worlds and social behaviors of persons who differ
in self-esteem. Persons high in their own self-estimation approach tasks and
persons with the expectation that they will be well-received and successful"
(p. 70). Similar findings of other researchers (Irwin, 1967; Rosenberg,
1965, 1968, 1979; Ziller, 1973) show that individuals high in self-esteem are
more independent of external reinforcement and more consistent in their
social behavior.

Research also provides evidence that persons with negative self-
regard tend to be more destructive, more anxious, more stressful, and
more likely to manifest psychosomatic symptoms than people of average or
high self-regard. Although *feeling* worthless is not the same as *being*
worthless, its impact on student behavior is often the same. "I never raise
my hand in class," a high-school student wrote. "I guess it goes back to
elementary school; when I asked my teacher about a question, she responded, 'Oh, that's the easiest problem in the chapter; any dummy could
figure that out.'" Whether intentional or unintentional, a disinviting comment can have lasting and devastating results on self-esteem.

What research findings and student reports on the importance of
self-regard mean for educators is that many common classroom problems
such as student disruption, inattention, apathy, and anxiety probably indicate negative self-regard on the part of the students exhibiting such behavior. Research on classroom discipline (Branch, Damico, and Purkey,

1977) reveals a significant relationship between students' low self-concepts as learners and their misbehavior in the classroom.

The Branch et al. study (1977) evaluated disruptive and nondisruptive middle-school students (grades five through eight) on their professed and inferred academic self-concepts. Analysis revealed significant differences between the two groups. Those students identified by their behavior as disruptive had significantly lower self-concepts as learners than did students identified as nondisruptive. The theoretical implication drawn from the study was that students' negative feelings about themselves as learners may be a contributing factor in student disruption. Related research in the area of juvenile delinquency has indicated a strong relationship between negative self-concept and delinquency. Self-concept may eventually prove to be a significant mediating variable that will help us understand many types of seemingly unrelated behavior problems.

Compounding the problem of negative self-regard is the apparent correlation between a person's self-regard and the degree to which he or she is disturbed by the poor opinion of others. Rosenberg (1965) asked a sample of high-school students how much it bothered them to discover that others held them in low regard. By comparing answers with self-esteem scores, Rosenberg found that the lower a student's self-regard, the more that student was upset by the negative opinions of others. Such students are highly sensitive to the behavior of others toward them, and their feelings can remain injured for many years, creating a downward spiraling effect on self-regard.

One teacher revealed the long-term impact of real or imagined slights thus:

> Several years ago a young man, now the assistant manager of a large grocery store, stopped me at the counter and said: "You don't remember me, do you?" I replied that I remembered his face and that he had been a student of mine. Since at least ten years had passed, I could not remember his name. His remark that followed stunned me. I did not try to argue or insist that I had never said it. Instead I said: "I only hope that I never said such a thing to you or to any other student. I hope you are doing well." I walked away, wondering if I were guilty, if I had—in disgust, anger, or frustration—said it. I made a commitment never to let it happen again. This is what the assistant manager told me I said to him: "Right before I quit school, you told me that I'd never amount to anything. You see, I've proved you wrong."

Behavior is determined by subjective perceptions; whether a teacher's disinviting message is real or imagined, it has the potential to take on a life of its own and exist for many years, particularly in the minds of students already unsure of their own worth and ability.

Summary

In this chapter we have explored two foundations of invitational education: the perceptual tradition and the self-concept theory. The perceptual tradition was explained to emphasize the individual's world of experience, the learning of personal reality, and the ability to reflect upon perceptions. Self-concept theory was presented to show how a person's self-concept develops primarily from inviting or disinviting messages sent, received, and acted upon. We have also explained in this chapter that each person has a strong tendency to protect his or her self-concept against conflicting pressures, to think as well of oneself as circumstances permit, and to want to be regarded positively by significant others. Chapter 3 examines the perceptions of educators and sets the stage for the concrete strategies and procedures of invitational education presented in Chapters 4 and 5.

Chapter Three

THE INVITING APPROACH

An idea whose time has come: the gradually formed and tested hypothesis that the individual has within himself vast resources for self-understanding, for altering his self-concept, his attitudes, and his self-directed behavior—and that these resources can be tapped if only a definable climate of facilitative psychological attitudes can be provided.

Carl Rogers
"In Retrospect—Forty-Six Years"
American Psychologist
(1974, p. 115)

To be optimally inviting, personally and professionally, it is important for educators to have an understanding of the perceptual tradition and self-concept theory and to apply this understanding to real-world situations involving specific people and their endless quests for self-esteem. This involves the artful blending of *teacher perception, teacher stance,* and *teacher behavior* into what we call a *theory of practice.* These three components are now examined in turn.

Teacher Perception

And now here is my secret, a very simple secret:
It is only with the heart that one can see rightly,
What is essential is invisible to the eye.
Antoine de Saint-Exupéry
The Little Prince
(1943, p. 87)

Any teacher who has been in classrooms for any length of time knows that teaching is a fragile, sometimes puzzling, process. Things can go well when least expected, and the best-prepared lesson can fail. The answer to the question of why a class succeeds or fails is likely to be found in the teacher's perceptions. As explained in Chapter 2, people behave according to the particular beliefs they hold about themselves, others, and the world. This process has been documented by Combs (1982), Giorgi (1970), Kranz, Weber, and Fishell (1970), Wasicsko (1977), and others. When teachers believe that students are able, valuable, and responsible—and when they view teaching as the process of inviting students to see themselves in essentially positive ways—they are well on their way to becoming invitational professionals, with beliefs and behaviors of the type advocated in this book.

The importance of being able to see positive attributes in students that students may not otherwise see in themselves is explained by Pullias (1975):

One of the greatest functions of a teacher is to give his
students a "vision of greatness," which is a figurative way
of saying a clear picture of their potential as human beings
and of the possibility of realizing that which they can be.
. . . The individual cannot or will not see and take advantage
of opportunity, however physically available it may be,
unless he is brought to believe that he has possibilities for
growth and that this opportunity is a door for him.
(p. 173)

No single explanation, of course, can cover the entire complex of teaching and learning. It is increasingly evident, however, that the teacher's perceptions of students, as reflected in his or her behavior, have the power to influence how students view themselves and how well they learn in school. As Jourard (1968) explained: "The teacher who turns on the dull student, the coach who elicits a magnificent performance from someone of whom it could not be expected, are people who themselves have an image of the pupils' possibilities; and they were effective in realizing their images" (p. 126). Like a sculptor who envisions something in a block of marble that others cannot see, the inviting teacher perceives possibilities in students that others miss.

The studies that have focused most directly on the perceptions of professional helpers include those of Combs (1972), Combs et al. (1978), Combs, Soper, Gooding, Benton, Dickman, and Usher (1969), O'Roark (1974), and Wasicsko (1977). In a series of research studies spanning more than a decade, Combs and associates investigated the ways in which successful teachers and other professional helpers organize their perceptions of themselves, others, and the world. The research also investigated the ways in which these perceptual organizations influence effectiveness in helping others. Combs reported that effective helpers in many professions, including teaching, counseling, nursing, the ministry, and public service, can be distinguished from less effective helpers on the basis of their perceptions. He concluded that a high degree of similarity exists among the belief systems of "good helpers" in numerous profession fields. Good teachers, for example, may be clearly identified from poor ones on the basis of their perceptions of people as able rather than unable, friendly rather than unfriendly, worthy rather than unworthy, dependable rather than undependable, helpful rather than hindering, and internally, rather than externally, motivated (Combs et al., 1969). From these and other studies (Koffman, 1975; Usher and Hanke, 1971; Wasicsko, 1977), it appears that the ways in which teachers and other helpers perceive students will heavily influence their success or failure in teaching.

Research is now providing ample evidence to support two important assumptions of invitational education. First, inviting and disinviting messages primarily result from teacher perceptions. Second, these messages play a significant role in affecting students' self-concepts as well as their attitudes toward school, the relationships they form in school, and their school achievement. Clearly, it is important for teachers to work on developing positive perceptions of their students, themselves, and education if they wish to be a beneficial presence in the lives of students. Positive perceptions means viewing students as able, valuable, and responsible as well as seeing oneself and education in essentially favorable ways. These teacher perceptions are worth considering in greater detail.

Viewing Students as Able

I'll give you the one thing you don't have! A diploma—A Ph.T.—A Doctor of Thinkology!

The Wizard to the Scarecrow
Screenplay by Noel Langley, Florence Ryerson, and Edgar Allan Woolf
The Wizard of Oz
(Metro-Goldwyn-Mayer, 1939)

As presented in Chapter 1, an important assumption of invitational education is that each student has relatively untapped capabilities for thinking, choosing, and learning, and that these capabilities can be realized in an optimally inviting environment. This assumption is supported by what is known about the capabilities of children.

From the moment of birth, infants are marvelously curious, seeming to obtain a sense of pleasure and satisfaction from understanding and mastering their environments. From a very young age, children rapidly acquire knowledge, which they apply to gain further understanding of their environments.

Today we know that children possess far greater capacities for learning than almost anyone previously had thought possible. Human intelligence is currently recognized as a dynamic potential, rather than a static entity. Simply defined, intelligence is the level of mental functioning that is reflected in the quality or effectiveness of an individual's behavior. This level of mental functioning can be strongly influenced by either facilitating or debilitating environments. For example, research by Bloom (1976) and associates has documented that most students develop a desire for further learning when they are provided with favorable learning conditions. In concluding his extensive review of the research on the relationship between intelligence and experience, Hunt (1961) commented: "It is highly unlikely that any society has developed a system of child rearing and education that maximizes the potential of the individuals which compose it. Probably no individual has ever lived whose full potential for happy intellectual interest and growth has been achieved" (p. 346). Human potential, although not always apparent, is always there, waiting to be discovered and invited forth.

Throughout their school years, some students become more creative, some less so; some become excited about learning, some become bored and disillusioned; some become intellectually active, some less active. Some students fall in love with books, others learn to hate them. Some develop a passion for physical exercise, others learn to avoid it. The entire process is heavily influenced by the belief systems of teachers as manifested in inviting or disinviting behavior.

In addition to their actual classroom presence, students exist as mental images in the minds of teachers. Teachers who believe that certain children cannot learn or benefit from instruction will have little success in teaching them. As Childs emphasized years ago, if we believe that half the people cannot think for themselves, and if we behave accordingly, we will establish a school system that will actually make it impossible for half of the people to think for themselves (Childs, 1931).

Happily, when teachers have positive views of students' abilities, students are likely to respond in positive ways. This process has been documented by Good (1981), Good, Biddle, and Brophy (1975), Good and Brophy (1978), Insel and Jacobson (1975), Jones and Panitch (1971), Rubovits and Maehr (1971), and others. It was also described by a student who wrote: "I am 21 and a painting major. When I was in the sixth grade, I suggested a mural design for our school. My teacher was so pleased she ordered the paint, ladder, even excused me from regular class so I could complete the mural. I usually tire of my past work, or don't think it's very good, yet I still believe that mural was one of the best paintings I've ever done. I think it turned out so well because the teacher had such faith in my ability." Students develop best when they share the company of teachers who see them as possessing relatively untapped abilities in myriad areas, and who invite them to realize their potential.

Perceiving Students as Valuable

It has been a very great pleasure to make your acquaintance.
Mrs. Kendall to Merrick
Bernard Pomerance
The Elephant Man
(1979, p. 34)

When educators believe that each student is a person of value, their behavior will reflect this belief. As Hall (1959) explained, people constantly communicate their real feelings in the "silent language," the language of behavior. When teachers perceive their students positively they are more likely to involve themselves with their students, both personally and professionally, and a *doing with,* as opposed to a *doing to,* process often results. The warmth of this teacher–student partnership is illustrated by a middle-school student who wrote, "Mr. McFayden is my best teacher, and he asked me to remind him to watch his weight—and I do, too!" Education is, or should be, a cooperative enterprise. An atmosphere of mutual respect and positive regard increases the likelihood of cooperation and student success in school. This atmosphere is particularly important in working with students identified as disadvantaged.

According to Brophy's research (1975), the most effective teachers of disadvantaged or minority group students are those who stress the unique value of the individual student. Such teachers are sensitive to the fact that children show uneven patterns of achievement and that standardized test scores for groups of children do not necessarily indicate a particular child's general mental ability. These teachers understand that comparison of students can be perceived as very disinviting, particularly for those who are told again and again, both verbally and nonverbally, that they are *less* able, *less* valuable, *less* responsible than their more advantaged peers.

Unfortunately, positive attitudes toward disadvantaged students seem to be in short supply in some schools. Research indicates that many teachers hold lower expectations for the performance of disadvantaged students (Soares and Soares, 1970); they are likely to behave differently and inappropriately toward these students, by refusing them sufficient time to answer questions or rewarding them for inappropriate behavior (Good, 1980; Good and Brophy, 1977), and tend to provide them with fewer verbal and nonverbal reinforcements (Friedman and Friedman, 1973). These and other findings indicate that if teachers are to be personally and professionally inviting, it is vital that they develop and maintain a positive view of all students.

One bonus in seeing students as valuable is that such a view will probably contribute significantly to the mental health of students. As early as 1947, Fromm pointed out that feelings of worthlessness characterize the sick personality. Similar conclusions were presented by Moustakas (1966). Listing ways in which educators contribute to the development of self-esteem, Moustakas first listed the importance of confirming the student as being of noncomparable and nonmeasureable worth. Teachers signal their positive beliefs in countless ways. One student wrote: "My third grade teacher . . . I was new in the school (in the middle of the year) and was lonely, shy, alone. It was a cold, winter day and I had a cold. I sneezed very hard and didn't have a tissue. I tried to hide it in my hand, in a fist. Mrs. Benedict very tactfully brought me a tissue and slipped it in my hand. I was *very* thankful." When teachers believe in the value of each student, they telegraph this belief in everything they do and every way they do it.

Seeing Students as Responsible

Humanistic psychology has the virtue of fitting what seems to be an enduring and universal value of human life—a regard for individual responsibility.

Irvin L. Child
Humanistic Psychology and the Research Tradition
(1973, p. 17)

In North American schools today, the number of things a student can be ordered or coerced to do is, or should be, kept to a minimum. Because most student behavior cannot be forced to occur, the inviting or disinviting messages received by students take on the great importance of influencing what students elect to do.

From an inviting perspective, there is no way that a teacher can "learn" a student. Students choose to learn, just as they choose *not* to learn in the face of ridicule, embarrassment, or coercion. Invitational education builds on the assumption that students will elect to learn those things they perceive to be significant in their personal lives. What teachers can do, therefore, is conduct themselves and their classes so that students are consistently invited to perceive the significance of course content, to choose meaningful programs, to cooperate in the learning process, and to participate actively in school activities.

Teachers who recognize the definite limits of their powers to make students learn are in a good position to try alternative ways of teaching. They can more easily find their own best ways of inviting students to discover the personal pleasure of self-directed learning. For example, a Minnesota high-school science teacher was so successful at inviting students to learn science that some students continued to attend his class even after dropping out of school! One such "drop-in" en route to this science class was intercepted by a secretary, who demanded to know why this drop-out was in the building. The science teacher, overhearing the question, quietly took the secretary aside and said, "Our job is not to ask students why they're here; our job is to ask them why they're not here." Several days later, the principal asked another of the teacher's drop-ins why he continued to attend class. The boy responded, "Frankly, I just want to see what he's gonna do next!"

By respecting students and believing in their ability, value, and self-directing powers, teachers can spend less time in trying to force students to learn, and more energy in developing an exciting and appealing environment for learning to occur. Leo Buscaglia, a colleague of ours, offered a beautiful analogy of how this might be accomplished. Buscaglia used the metaphor of knowledge being a marvelous feast. What the teacher can do is prepare food with great relish and care, sample it frequently, dance around the table at mealtime, and invite students to join the celebration! This approach seems to make better sense than trying to force-feed unwilling students—and is certainly more fun.

Available research by DeCharms (1968, 1972), Lepper and Greene (1975), Maehr (1974), Mahoney (1974), and others seems to support the idea that choice and feelings of personal responsibility promote school achievement. Further, perceived choice and responsibility tend to result in more student receptivity to rules and procedures (Tjosvold, 1977; Tjosvold and Santamaria, 1977). Mahoney (1974) reported that students tend to be happier and to accomplish greater academic success when they can make significant choices in their daily schedule of activities. According to Mahoney, these results hold true even when self-imposed responsibilities are the same as those previously imposed by teachers. The apparent rule is that when students are given meaningful choices in their education they are likely to learn more, for they are learning what they have elected to learn.

The importance of personal choice is also evident in areas other than education. As early as 1960, Lippitt and White demonstrated through experimentally controlled social climates the value of leaders who encouraged self-direction in workers. This finding has been supported by more recent research by Notz (1975) and others indicating the importance of workers' feelings of autonomy in their work activities. Human behavior results from a vast array of possible modes of thought, and people tend to value what they do when they believe they have some choice in doing it.

Finally, a belief in the ability of people to make intelligent choices is the foundation of democracy. When Thomas Jefferson wrote the Declaration of Independence, he never wavered in his faith that people, when free to choose, will find their own best ways. He believed that if individuals were unable to handle freedom of choice, the remedy was not to take it away from them but to "inform them by education" (Wagoner, 1976, p. 5). When students are encouraged to make significant choices in their lives they are far more likely, later in life, to maintain personal integrity in the face of external pressure and manipulation. They are also more likely, we believe, to support a democratic philosophy of government.

Teachers are in a better position to facilitate student responsibility when they hold certain perceptions about themselves.

Viewing Oneself Positively

I to myself am dearer than a friend.
Shakespeare
Two Gentlemen of Verona
Act II, Scene vi

Perceiving students as valuable, able, and responsible is much easier when teachers have a positive and realistic view of themselves. A growing body of literature in the fields of education and psychology centers on the assumption that when teachers better understand, accept, and like themselves, they have a much greater capacity to understand, accept, and like students. Researchers have reported significant relationships between teacher self-regard and such factors as how they evaluate students (Curtis and Altman, 1977; Drugger, 1971), how effective they tend to be as teachers (Noad, 1979; Usher and Hanke, 1971), how well students see themselves (Landry, 1974), and how well students achieve on standardized tests (Aspy and Buhler, 1975). Emerging evidence indicates that a positive, realistic view of oneself is an important ingredient in behaving in an inviting manner. "Mrs. Reynolds expected good things of us," a high-school student wrote, "and we could tell she also expected good things of herself."

The ability to speak to oneself about oneself in positive, realistic ways is an important aspect of invitational education. To understand this, imagine two science teachers. Both possess essentially the same knowledge and skills. During each teacher's class, two students carry on a private conversation, ignoring the carefully prepared demonstration by the teacher. This student behavior elicits different *internal dialogues* (what we say to ourselves about ourselves, sometimes called *self-talk*) from the two teachers. The first teacher thinks: "I've stayed up half the night to prepare this demonstration, and those two students are not paying a bit of attention to me. I know I'm not the greatest teacher, but why do kids have to be so rude?" The second teacher, faced with exactly the same student behavior, is more positive and realistic and thinks something like this: "Those two students are not paying attention. That's too bad, because this is an important and well-prepared demonstration. I'll try to find additional ways to make these demonstrations more interesting. Meanwhile, after class I'll tell them that their lack of attention is disturbing me."

The first teacher's perception and internal dialogue are self-defeating. They exaggerate the meaning of the student's behavior, they emphasize the lack of attention of two students over the attention of all the other students in the class, and they overgeneralize the situation by assuming personal inadequacy. Clearly, the first teacher's internal dialogue is inappropriate, anxiety-producing, and self-defeating. The second teacher makes a more positive appraisal of the classroom situation and forms a more positive and constructive pattern of internal self-statements.

Awareness of one's internal dialogue and realistic appraisals of classroom experiences have been stressed by numerous researchers who report that what people say internally about themselves plays an important role in their adaptive or maladaptive behavior (Meichenbaum, 1974; Thomas, 1982). In Mahoney's (1975) words, we need to "clean up what we say about ourselves" (p. 865). Teachers are too often overly critical in what they say to themselves about themselves. "The worst enemies of teachers," as one teacher noted, "are teachers!" An important way to become more personally and professionally inviting, therefore, is to be gentle with oneself and to practice a pattern of positive and productive self-statements.

Perceiving oneself positively also means applying the categories *valuable, able,* and *responsible* to one's own existence. The perception that people are worthy of inviting, that they have relatively untapped potential, and that they are able to make meaningful choices in their lives applies to oneself as well as to others. Positive and realistic perceptions of the self are essential parts of the inviting approach to education. Now let us consider teacher perceptions of education.

Perceiving Education Affirmatively

In teaching, we do not impose our wills on students, but introduce them to many mansions of the heritage in which we ourselves strive to live, and to the improvement of which we ourselves are dedicated.

Israel Scheffler
"Philosophical Models of Teaching"
In R. S. Peters (Ed.), The Concept of Education
(1967, p. 134)

Teaching is a delicate relationship between and among people. It involves knowing something worth knowing and desiring to share and extend this knowledge with others. Educators who are personally and professionally inviting not only have positive perceptions about themselves and others, they also, as Wasicsko (1977) has documented, have rich and extensive perceptions about the subjects they desire to teach. One student said, "Because Mr. Chambers opened up so many doors of knowledge to us, I felt smarter and eager to learn." Such teachers invite students to participate in the enterprise of inquiry.

Involved in the process of extending invitations to learning is the teacher's personal relationship to the content and essence of what he or she teaches. As Pine and Boy (1979) point out, it is important for teachers to grow in and through their teaching. A teacher who can perceive meaning, clarity, significance, and excitement in what he or she teaches is better able to invite students to do likewise. In addition, the likelihood of an invitation to learning being accepted is increased when the teacher is perceived as having expertise, enthusiasm, and sound judgment, as well as being seen as trustworthy and caring. These student perceptions are most likely to emerge when the teacher develops and maintains a particular stance.

Teacher Stance

I want you to meet my needs.
For you to be willing to do so, I must give you a reason for doing so.
It therefore follows that I can only meet my needs after I have first considered yours.
I have learned then that I can start out being as selfish as I like, but I cannot achieve my goal without considering how others will respond.
Walter Lifton
Working with Groups
(1962, p. 21)

Although invitational education is based on perceptions, it is a theory of practice. Thus, an inviting or disinviting message is an action—to exist, an invitation must be manifested. People are not invited to realize their potential simply because we think good thoughts, or destroyed because we wish them ill. To make a difference, perceptions must be embodied in a consistent behavioral framework. We call this framework a *stance,* to indicate the general position from which one operates and one's typical pattern of action. When stance is manifested in a positive sense, it is the prevailing disposition to be a beneficial presence in the lives of people. It is epitomized by one teacher who commented, "My job is to help children understand how good they are and how much they can learn."

An inviting stance seems to have at least four basic qualities: *intentionality, respect, direction,* and *responsibility.* Let us now look at each of these four qualities.

Intentionality

Man's vitality is as great as his intentionality; they are interdependent.
Paul Tillich
The Courage to Be
(1952, p. 81)

Invitational education does not happen by accident. It is intentionally created by people who want to develop such an approach to learning and who commit themselves to doing so. Intentionality, as defined by Rollo May (1969), is a statement of "commitment and convictions" (p. 230). In developing an inviting stance an educator intends that his or her actions summon people to realize their potential. As Ivey (1968) states, "the individual who acts with intentionality is not bound to one course of action, but can act in the moment to respond to ever changing environmental situations" (p. 58). Thus, the intentionally inviting professional is someone with a directed but flexible plan—someone who does things on purpose and for reasons he or she can explain or defend.

Being intentional when working with people enables an educator to be dependable, but not narrowly predictable, in his or her actions. With a dependable stance, one's actions become more trustworthy in the eyes of others, and are less likely to be perceived as containing hidden agendas. Thus, intentionality is an important quality of the inviting stance.

Respect

Let people realize clearly that every time they threaten someone or humiliate or hurt unnecessarily or dominate or reject another human being, they become forces for the creation of psychopathology, even if these be small forces. Let them recognize that every man who is kind, helpful, decent, psychologically democratic, affectionate, and warm, is a psychotherapeutic force even though a small one.
Abraham H. Maslow
Motivation and Personality
(1970, p. 254)

A second quality of an inviting stance is respect. Involved in developing and maintaining an inviting stance is the basic notion that the *sender* understands and respects the right of the *receiver* to accept, reject, or hold in abeyance any message received. This care is communicated by respecting the *net,* the hypothetical boundary between sender and receiver that marks the personal, inviolable territory of each human.

Educators who maintain an inviting stance realize they cannot cross the net. Recognizing the net, they consistently choose to act, both personally and professionally, in a manner that reflects respect for others. Application of this basic principle of invitational education means that whatever else a school should be, it should not be a place where people are embarrassed, insulted, or humiliated. If there are policies, practices, or programs that cannot be performed in accordance with respectful treatment, or if there are faculty or staff who cannot or will not function in a consistently respectful manner, they should not be in schools. With these criteria in mind, demeaning school practices such as public ridicule, invidious comparisons, deliberate humiliation, and corporal punishment must be eliminated if a school is to consider itself personally and professionally inviting. This brings us to the third quality of an inviting stance—direction.

Direction

Each act of consciousness tends toward something, it is a turning of the person toward something, and has within it, no matter how latent, some push toward a direction for action.

Rollo May
Love and Will
(*1969, p. 230*)

Every inviting action involves direction—the coming together for some worthwhile purpose. Coming together is not something obtained through an act of will, although the *desire* to reach this special state is paramount. Coming together involves a sensitivity to ourselves and others and a keen awareness of the specific situations in which people find themselves. Human beings seem to have a deep desire to come together, although it is difficult to describe in words. Chamberlain (1981) has called this desire "juncturing." People seem to know when they have reached this point: something seems to click—it feels right. On the other hand, people seem to know when it is lacking—things seem mechanical, artificial, disjointed, out of focus. There is no real contact point. Its lack is reflected in such comments as "I can't reach that student," "She seems to be somewhere else," or "He's just not with me."

Educators who maintain an inviting stance seek to come together with others in mutually beneficial ways. They also seek to find a special feeling of "withness" within themselves and with nature. Withness may not always be reached, but is worth seeking. Coming together—sharing thoughts and activities—can be one of life's most enjoyable experiences.

Responsibility

Man must realize himself not within himself but in a responsible and loving relation to his fellowmen.

Reinhold Niebuhr
Faith and History: A Comparison of Christian and Modern Views of History
(*1949, p. 197*)

The fourth quality for developing and maintaining an inviting stance is responsibility. Inviting people to realize their potential is not something to be taken lightly. Because inviting and disinviting messages have the potential to influence the course of human development, it is imperative that educators understand and accept the responsibilities involved. Inviting and disinviting acts often are soon forgotten by the sender, but are not so easily forgotten by the recipient. As one student said, "I would rather have my teacher say 'no' than make all those phoney promises. She thinks just because we're students we don't remember anything."

An inviting stance always entails taking responsibility for one's actions. When an invitation is accepted and good things result, it increases the likelihood that future invitations will be accepted. Conversely, when an invitation is accepted and bad things result, it increases the probability that future invitations will be rejected. Therefore, it is important that educators not only send inviting messages in a responsible manner, but also take the responsibility for seeing that students have a reasonable chance of accepting and acting upon these invitations successfully.

Too often in schools we are less than responsible with our invitations. We invite students to be our guests for a learning feast. Yet once they accept our invitations, we sometimes insult them with invidious seating arrangements, bore them with bland and unappetizing food, speed up or slow down their eating with rigid time schedules, evaluate them on how much and how well they eat, and fail them when they make too many errors. Those who are not "eating up to grade level" are remanded to "remedial eating" where they may be served predigested food over and over until they consume a predetermined amount. Is it any wonder that after a few years many students are less than eager to accept our invitations?

Educators who are committed to an inviting stance are aware of their responsibilities. Having decided to be personally and professionally inviting, they work not only to invite but also to insure that desirable consequences occur as a result of the inviting process. They follow through on responsibilities incurred as a result of their actions.

Thus, invitational education, although based on perceptions, involves a particular stance: a commitment to act intentionally toward others and oneself in ways that reflect respect, direction, and responsibility.

Teacher Behavior

Once a stance is established, inviting behaviors can be exhibited in myriad ways. These ways include specific skills, which are presented in Chapter 4, as well as practical methods presented in Appendices A and B. This section on teacher behaviors examines choices embedded in every invitation: the choices of sending or not sending, of accepting or not accepting.

Invitational education involves choices, and choices by their very nature involve risks. Let us now examine the choices and concomitant risks involved in behaving in an inviting manner.

To Send or Not to Send

When I was a young girl, over thirty years ago, I attended a square dance. While there I spied a handsome young man standing alone. After watching him for awhile, I summoned my courage, walked over to him, and said: "Excuse me, sir, do you dance?" He replied "No, I don't know how." And I said: "I'll teach you!" We've been dancing together ever since . . . during our thirty years of marriage.

A graduate student
University of North Carolina—Greensboro

An invitation is a choice someone made, a risk someone took. Inviting others involves several risks: the risk of rejection, the risk of being misunderstood or misinterpreted, or the risk of being accepted but having things not work out as anticipated. Each of these risks can be minimized, but because we work with human beings in a less than totally certain world, risks will always be present. Would we really want it otherwise? The greatest hazards in life are to risk nothing, send nothing, accept nothing, be nothing.

Although we take risks when we invite, there are greater risks in not inviting. Take the case of friendship. A person can be a relative by chance, but friendship requires invitations. Our closest friends were once total strangers! Without inviting messages sent and received, they would have remained faces in the crowd. A life without friends seems too great a risk to pay for the security of not inviting.

Teachers who don't invite may be safe from rejection, misunderstanding, or involvement, but that's not how teachers should be. Students learn that they are able, valuable, and responsible when someone takes the risk of inviting them to feel that way. In the inviting process, good intentions are necessary but not sufficient. To be personally and professionally inviting, it is important to ask oneself: "Is this the most appropriate action I can take with this person at this time?"

Choosing to behave in an inviting manner does not mean constantly sending affirming messages. Sometimes the most inviting thing we can do is *not* send an invitation. For example, inviting a colleague to have a milkshake when you know he or she is trying to lose weight is at best thoughtless. An ill-timed, inappropriate, or thoughtless invitation is often perceived as very disinviting. Offering a banner to "the best-behaved class" would be appealing to primary-school children, but the same offer made in a junior high school would be received with horror!

In considering the risks involved in inviting or not inviting, there seem to be two general guidelines. The first is to *listen* and be sensitive to what might be perceived as appropriate and caring behavior, or as inappropriate and uncaring. Second, when the evidence seems about equally divided between sending or not sending—send! If we invite, others may accept; if we don't they can't. Older adults, when looking back over their lives, report that they worry more about the things they did *not* do, rather than the things they did (Bennett, 1982). We have a finite amount of time for inviting . . . we have eternity for not doing so.

To Accept or Not to Accept

And I'd like to thank everybody I ever met in my entire life.
Maureen Stapleton
Acceptance Speech for Best Supporting Actress
1982 Academy Awards

The inviting process is an interdependent activity. It involves alternating between sending and accepting. Just as there are risks in sending and not sending, so too are there risks in accepting and not accepting.

Accepting an invitation is another way of saying "I trust you." This trust involves a special risk of vulnerability. We don't have control over other people's trustworthiness, yet by accepting their invitations we are placing ourselves in their care. Ultimately, however, if we always choose control over risk, we run the even greater hazard described by Edgar Lee Masters in *Spoon River Anthology* (1922): "For love was offered me and I shrank from its disillusionment; sorrow knocked at my door, but I was afraid; ambition called to me, but I dreaded the chances. Yet all the while I hungered for meaning in my life" (p. 65). When chances of success are good, Masters seems to say, take the chance. He continues by saying "And now I know that we must lift the sail and catch the winds of destiny wherever they drive the boat" (1922, p. 65).

As we have seen, a guideline for accepting life's opportunities is a willingness to risk. The risk of living in a world where people avoid involvement seems greater than the risk of being hurt. Of course, there are reasons why certain invitations cannot or should not be accepted. A reasonable rule of thumb seems to be: accept those invitations worth accepting and decline the rest graciously. Even the process of not accepting an invitation can be done in an inviting manner.

Numerous surveys and interviews with teachers and students show that there appears to be a great variety of reasons why people do not accept invitations. Surprisingly, most of these reasons have nothing to do with rejecting the inviter! As a colleague, Lisa Hockaday, pointed out, not accepting an invitation does not necessarily mean rejection. By not accepting, some students are seeing if we are really sincere, or are seeking time to think things over. This seems especially true for students who have experienced much frustration and failure in schools. These are the students who are most likely to benefit from invitations, yet they are also the least likely to be invited and the most likely to have trouble accepting. Because these students have not received many invitations from the school in the past, they have a difficult time recognizing and accepting those few they may now receive. Often they mask their difficulty by pretending they do not want to be invited. Choosing to invite such students involves making an effort to know and understand their feelings and to recognize that nonacceptance does not mean rejection. It also means understanding that our present actions may make it easier for those students to accept invitations in the future.

We have only just begun to understand the dynamics of sending/not sending, accepting/not accepting. But in simple terms, it seems to go something like this:

> If I don't invite, you can't accept.
> If you can't accept, you won't invite.
> If you don't invite, I can't accept.
> If there are no invitations, there is no development.

In this chapter we have seen that the inviting approach is a blend of perception, stance, and behavior coming together to form a theory of practice: "a body of prescriptions to guide practice" (Moore, 1974, p. 10). Invitational education is to be judged on its empirical basis, moral defensibility, clarity, and usefulness in suggesting intelligent and imaginative ways of being a beneficial presence in the lives of human beings. Now let us see how invitational education might be related to a common concern of educators: discipline.

An Inviting Approach to Discipline

Maintaining good discipline has been, and probably always will be, a major concern of educators. Students tend to resist external control because it restricts personal choice and limits freedom. This love of individual freedom is a valuable part of the democratic ethic and should be cultivated rather than condemned. At the same time, teachers are responsible for maintaining reasonable control in the classroom and for achieving the goals set forth by society. To maintain order (usually called *discipline*), teachers have tried just about everything.

Earlier methods of discipline were essentially negative, and fear and punishment played dominant roles. One of the first schoolhouses built in the United States had a whipping post (Manning, 1959) and in the "good old days" many techniques were devised to inflict physical punishment on erring students. Fear, too, played a major role in maintaining discipline, and children received ominous warnings from home, school, and the pulpit that, as James Whitcomb Riley said in "Little Orphant Annie," "the gobble-uns'll git you ef you don't watch out!" (1916, p. 1170).

Fortunately, more modern methods of maintaining classroom discipline are generally positive. Charles (1981), Dollar (1972), Dreikurs and Cassel (1974), Holmes, Holmes, and Field (1974), Purkey and Avila (1971), Schmidt (in press), Sloane (1976), Williams and Kamala (1973), and others have provided many practical, humane tips on how to deal with misbehavior. Behavior modification techniques that attempt to reinforce desirable behavior and extinguish undesirable behavior are often effective. For behavior modification, the classroom is usually arranged so that when students behave in desirable ways, desirable things happen to them. Reinforcement of this sort relies primarily on rewards rather than punishments to modify and shape student behavior.

It should be noted, however, that both earlier and contemporary behavioral approaches treat discipline, whether rewarding or punishing, primarily as a matter of employing certain techniques. Invitational education, by comparison, focuses on the larger issues of teacher perception and teacher stance. The teacher strives to develop a positive perceptual orientation regarding self and others, and works to maintain discipline through a stance that imparts gentle but firm expectations for self and others.

An inviting approach to discipline centers on the dignity of people. Whether intentionally or unintentionally, teachers and other professionals sometimes run roughshod over the personal feelings of students. "My last name is Turley," a student wrote, "and my science teacher always called me 'Turkey' and laughed. At first I felt hurt, and now I'm just resentful." When teachers employ tasteless humor, ridicule, and lack of respect with students, it is not surprising that students reply in kind. Students are likely to do unto teachers as teachers do unto them. In practical terms this means that teachers should practice common courtesy and civility and encourage these practices in others. A colleague of ours, Robert "Buzz" Lee, believes this process is so important that he signs a "no-cut contract" with each of his students at the beginning of each semester. This contract stipulates that "I won't disinvite myself, I won't disinvite you. I will invite myself, I will invite you."

Students who are consistently treated with dignity and respect are less likely to cause problems in the classroom. Conversely, students who think that teachers are out to embarrass them and that the system is geared to convince them that they are worthless, unable, and irresponsible will find ways to rebel, disrupt, and seek revenge—as humans have always done in their discontent and resentment. This is powerfully illustrated by the words of Shakespeare's hunchback Richard: "And therefore, since I cannot prove a lover, to entertain these fair well-spoken days, I am determined to prove a villain, and hate the idle pleasures of these days" (*Richard III,* Act I, Scene i). When students feel disinvited they are likely to respond in kind. The rule is clear: disinvitations beget disinvitations.

Beyond manifesting respect for students, good discipline is developed and maintained by teachers who believe that teaching should be as interesting and involving as possible. When teachers recognize boredom as a causal agent in misbehavior, they are more likely to seek ways to make their teaching as engaging and exciting as possible. Discipline problems diminish when students are interested and involved.

Finally, the ability to invite good discipline depends on the teacher's perception about what constitutes misbehavior. These beliefs vary considerably from teacher to teacher, school to school, and year to year. In 1848, for example, a North Carolina high school listed as misbehaviors boys and girls playing together, girls wearing long fingernails, and boys neglecting to bow before going home! Today most educators agree that rules should be reasonable, enforceable, and educationally relevant. Too often in the past, teachers and principals attempted to enforce rules that were authoritarian, generally disinviting, and—like regulations against tight pants, short skirts, long hair, and jewelry—had little relevance to education. With fewer but more reasonable rules, fewer rules are likely to be broken.

By now one may be thinking, "I believe these things about discipline, but some students still insist on being disruptive." This is true. Even in heaven there were discipline problems. (Lucifer, light-filled son of the morning, had to be kicked out of class!) Some students resist any form of control, and some discipline problems will continue to exist even in the most inviting school environment. When misbehavior exceeds reasonable limits, teachers and other school personnel might ask themselves: "What is happening here? Is the student upset or ill? Are certain factors in the school, such as temperature, class size, or time of day, eliciting misbehavior? How does this student view himself or herself and others in the school? Does the misbehaving student need professional counseling or other psychological help?" When satisfactory answers to questions like these do not excuse the misbehavior, an appropriate consequence is necessary. But even then, what the teacher believes about penalties makes a great difference. If teachers believe that penalties should be humane and used sparingly, they will resort to temporary denial of student privilege rather than to corporal punishment or psychological warfare. Punishment should not give students the resentful feeling of being wronged. The object of a penalty is to encourage the student to reflect on the offense, recognize why it was inappropriate, and take appropriate steps to correct it (Levin, 1959, p. 64).

Much has been written about maintaining discipline in the classroom, but little about ways to *invite* good discipline. Traditionally, the maintenance of classroom discipline has relied on targeting misbehaviors and exacting penalties. Invitational education, by comparison, promotes the belief that the identification and acknowledgment of appropriate student behavior helps set a positive tone and encourages everyone to aim at more beneficial expectations and activities. For too long we have exonerated the disinviting behavior of some teachers, or the disinviting nature of some policies, by simply labeling students as discipline problems. Perhaps now is the time to consider the reasons for misbehavior and to recognize that an ounce of persuasion is worth a pound of coercion.

Summary

In this chapter we have seen that the inviting approach requires the artful blending of teacher perception, stance, and behavior. Teacher perception includes viewing students as able, valuable, and responsible, and seeing oneself and one's profession in essentially positive ways. The concept of stance, the position from which one operates, was shown to be built around the importance of intentionality, respect, direction, and responsibility. Finally, the discussion of teacher behavior explored the basic choices involved in inviting: sending/not sending, accepting/not accepting. The three qualities of perception, stance, and behavior was related to the common problem of classroom discipline. In the next chapter we offer a sequence of inviting skills.

INVITING SKILLS

The best teacher is one who, through establishing a personal relation, frees the student to learn. Learning can only take place in the student, and the teacher can only create the conditions for learning. The atmosphere created by a good interpersonal relationship is the major condition for learning.

C. H. Patterson
Humanistic Education
(1973, p. 98)

All educators are inviting from time to time, either intentionally or unintentionally, but those who are perceived by others as dependably inviting possess two important characteristics. First, they consistently send messages that reflect unconditional respect for the value, ability, and self-directing powers of those they seek to help. Second, they are skillful in the process. This chapter suggests a sequence of inviting skills.

Invitational education involves the blending of perception and stance into that behavior which is most appropriate for the varied situations in which professionals find themselves. Although no two teaching situations are ever the same, there are skills that teachers and other professionals can use before, during, and after interactions with students.

Some words of caution are necessary when considering skills and their development. As we have seen, being optimally inviting results from basic perceptions regarding oneself, others, and the world, and from the development and maintenance of an inviting stance. The skills offered in this chapter are to be considered in this context. They should not be automatically applied to every situation. Without this understanding there is always the danger, as researchers (Mahon and Altman, 1977; Plum, 1981) have pointed out, that behavioral skills can replace thoughtful dialogue in the interpersonal process.

Although skills can be overemphasized, there are a number of specific, interdependent skills of teaching that can be of tremendous value to educators. We believe that these skills can be learned and can be improved upon. We also believe that the creation of inviting schools requires teachers who have more, rather than fewer, skills. These skills are both useful in themselves as well as a means of systematically developing deeper understandings and more integrated behaviors. Let us now examine three basic skills of inviting: *being ready, being with,* and *following through.*

Being Ready

The scout motto Be Prepared is a good beginning for developing inviting skills, for being ready is a most important skill of invitational education. Two subskills involved in being ready are preparing the environment and preparing oneself.

Preparing the Environment

The school environment, as Deutsch (1963), Herbert (1974), and others have documented, is where the student's positive or negative attitudes toward learning evolve. Students receive constant signals from the physical setting of schools, signals that tell them how much the people who design, build, operate, and maintain schools care about them and their learning. One student, describing her school, put it this way: "Yuk! How would you like to spend your whole day in a place that looks like this?"

As Russell, Purkey and Siegel (1982) have argued, preparing an inviting environment involves creating a clean, comfortable, and safe setting in which people who work in schools feel welcome and at ease. Everything in the school counts. Developing an optimal physical environment means working to insure that rooms, hallways, and commons areas are adequately lighted and heated, have plenty of fresh air, comfortable furniture, living plants, and attractive bulletin boards, and are freshly painted. (An often overlooked but particularly disinviting aspect of schools can be noisy, flourescent lights that keep buzzing in your head even after you leave the room.) Adequate supplies are also important, as one teacher explained in this vignette: "One of my five-year-olds is left-handed. Last week I overheard a discussion he had with another student over the importance of having left-handed scissors and cutting well. He then proceeded to ask, 'Mrs. Mancino, didn't you buy those left-handed scissors just for me?' Even left-handed scissors can be a special sort of invitation." Educators who understand and practice the inviting approach find ways to improve the physical environment, even in the face of the comment "There is nothing that can be done about the problem."

Berger and Luckman (1966) have noted that people both create and are created by their environments. An excellent example of a physically inviting school is Lancashire Elementary School in Wilmington, Delaware. Just a few of the things principal Fred Michaels and his staff have done include constructing a large sign welcoming everyone to the school, planting a tree *inside* the school, making one of the hallways into a cave museum, having students bring bricks and build their own road in a side corridor, and decorating the teachers' lounge so that it looks better than most restaurants. Even with these accomplishments, Fred Michaels has said, "We've only just begun!" Another example of a physically inviting school is Celoron Elementary School in Celoron, New York. Charlie Brown, the principal, organized parents and together they dug a beautiful swimming pool in the basement of a sixty-year-old school. Lancashire and Celoron schools are excellent illustrations of people preparing the environment to develop the most inviting place in town.

Preparing Oneself

It is probably impossible for a teacher to be dependably inviting unless he or she wants to be. Although not all of the reasons for wanting to invite are known, this desire seems to stem from a belief system based on the memory of one's own personal inviting or disinviting experiences. Being an inviting teacher probably involves the recollection and reflection on what it was like to be an invited, or disinvited, student.

Teachers can be prepared to be inviting to all students, especially those from different backgrounds, by examining their own presuppositions. Braun (1976) emphasizes that one of the most important things that teachers can do in the classroom is become aware of their own biases and stereotypes toward certain students, thus recognizing the influence of these perceptions on the academic performance of students. Teachers who seek to be objective in dealing with students may be looking for something that does not exist, for it is highly unlikely that people can be totally objective about anything of consequence. At the same time, stereotypes and biases can be recognized and taken into account when dealing with students of varying backgrounds. Inviting skills are more likely to be successful when teachers are honest with themselves about their own feelings and work to remove negative ones.

Dependably inviting teachers work at assessing their biases and then seek ways in which they can develop greater respect for individual differences and cultural diversity. Some ways of accomplishing this include attending workshops and ethnic festivals, and participating in various human relations programs. The result may be greater sensitivity and selectivity in choosing curriculum material. The result may also be more appropriate and caring phrases, examples, jokes, and stories used in the classroom, teachers' lounge, or wherever professionals gather. With such opportunities available for preparing oneself, there is no justification for the professional to be intentionally disinviting.

Being With

We stress throughout this book that being inviting is a special way of being with people. After adequate preparation of the physical environment and the self, teachers who desire to be personally and professionally inviting work to develop the following seven subskills: (1) developing trust, (2) reaching each student, (3) reading situations, (4) making invitations attractive, (5) insuring delivery, (6) negotiating, and (7) handling rejection. Each of these will be considered in turn.

Developing Trust

You can know me truly only if I let you, only if I want you to know me. If you want me to reveal myself, just demonstrate your good will—your will to employ your powers for my good, and not for my destruction.

Sidney Jourard
The Transparent Self
(1964, p. 5)

Invitations are most likely to be extended and accepted in an atmosphere of trust. Teachers who wish to become more personally and professionally inviting develop this trusting atmosphere by consistently behaving in a positive and dependable manner. This involves maintaining a warm, caring relationship with students, one in which teachers are able to be "real" with themselves and others.

The importance of warmth and care is documented by the findings of the National Association of Secondary School Principals, which collected opinions of high-school students (Sabine, 1971). One of the characteristics the students mentioned most often as typical of the best teacher was the quality of caring. Teachers communicate this caring behavior, as Mehrabian (1970, 1972, 1981) demonstrated, by such behaviors as listening without interrupting, facing the speaker squarely, and looking the person in the eye. The teacher who says "Of course I have time to talk with you" while continuing to grade papers is making a mockery of those words. Warmth and care are communicated by yielding interest and taking the time to listen.

In addition, it is important that teachers develop trust by respecting a student's confidentiality and following through on agreements. One betrayal of trust can destroy the best relationship. This was expressed to us by a graduate student: "When I was in high school I went to my football coach and shared my feelings about a personal matter. He seemed to listen and respect what I had to say, but at the next practice he kept bringing it up in front of the other guys. I'll never forgive him for that." Once a confidence is violated, it is difficult to re-establish a trusting relationship.

Trust is communicated with a person's entire body. Many researchers have provided ample evidence that we constantly communicate our real feelings with the language of behavior. With every verbal message (for example, "Welcome to the fifth grade"), there is also the behavioral message. The nonverbal message may lie in the teacher's tone of voice, physical appearance, body stance, facial expression, gestures, and physical proximity. Eye contact—looking directly at a particular student—especially can signal, "I am sincere in what I say, and my welcome is especially for you." A warm tone of voice, a neat physical appearance, a friendly smile, and direct eye contact all communicate that the student really *is* welcome. On the other hand, a teacher's aloof behavior, forced smile, tightly crossed arms, or indifferent manner may say more clearly than words, "I would rather not be here with you." Nonverbal language is so important that a hallmark of teachers who are dependably inviting is that they ensure that their eye contact, body posture, facial expression, and tone of voice agree with their verbal messages. For example, they look serious when stating displeasure, they look at a student when expressing sincerity, and they tense their bodies when expressing frustration. Their body language agrees with their spoken language.

Because students are quick to spot conflicts between what teachers say and how they behave, it is vital for inviting teachers, in Kraft's (1975) words, to "come on straight." Coming on straight means sharing feelings of happiness, anger, enthusiasm, sadness, excitement, or boredom. Teachers who are able to express their true feelings are more likely to be seen as "real" by students. One high-school student expressed the importance of "real" behavior in a teacher with these words: "I remember that our high-school history teacher was not afraid to express his feelings. He let us know when our misbehavior was getting to him. But he didn't show just his angry side. Once he cried at the end of a movie shown in class when the hero died. I learned a lot from him besides history . . . that it's OK for a man to express an emotion besides anger."

Coming on straight does not mean unbridled self-disclosure. Obvious advantages are involved in self-disclosure and sharing one's feelings with others, but such sharing should not be overdone. Disclosure, as Derlega and Chaikin (1975) emphasize, should be appropriate to the situation. When others casually ask how we are, they usually do not expect a complete medical history. Accepting and applying an inviting approach does not consist of displaying one's every immediate emotion. Just because we may *feel* like being intentionally disinviting does not mean we should be. In other words, coming on straight means taking the total situation into account when displaying feelings, and choosing behaviors that are caring and appropriate to the circumstances.

Self-disclosure is also determined by how comfortable we feel in revealing ourselves to others. We vary in how much we choose to share. Some teachers are more "open" than others. It is important, therefore, that teachers take their own feelings into account when determining how much of themselves they choose to share with other people and how skilled they will be in the process.

Perhaps the best way to summarize the importance of being real with students is to quote the words of a classroom teacher: "During the real 'up tight' period of the school year following Christmas vacation, I found a note under my classroom door. It read: 'Mr. Maggor, be yourself, don't try to be someone you're not.' It was signed 'A student and a friend.' Suddenly I realized that I had been coming down hard and mean on little things, which was not me and not my usual behavior. Later the two students, neither of whom I had in class, stopped by and talked with me about it. That day I learned a lot about the importance of being myself with my students." It is fortunate that teachers are not the only ones capable of being real and that many teachers will accept invitations as well as send them.

Reaching Each Student

It is not enough simply to send inviting messages. Invitations are a means for personally involving each student in his or her education. Teachers who practice invitational education ensure that their invitations to learning are distributed fairly and received by each student. As mentioned earlier, most teachers tend to communicate a disproportionate number of invitations to some students while neglecting others. The problem of favoritism and its negative influences on both self-concept and school achievement has been documented by House and More (1974) and Insel and Jacobson (1975).

One way to reduce or eliminate favoritism is to send invitations to learning systematically. Rather than relying on a random pattern of interaction in which the teacher will most likely call on those students perceived as having the correct answer, the inviting teacher works to ensure that each student is summoned cordially to participate in class. This is accomplished through rotating assignments, seating charts, class rosters, check sheets, card files, or other means. The teacher's attention is equally spread and time is taken for some personal contact with each student each day. Appendix A offers some practical techniques for accomplishing this.

It is difficult to overestimate the importance of the time reserved for one-on-one contacts with individual students. Although it is not easy with large classes, it is vital that the teacher squeeze in a few moments for semiprivate chats. These chats may last less than a minute, but they can be powerful invitations to learning. Inviting teachers use odd bits and pieces of time for these brief talks (while waiting for the bell, walking to the car, serving on lunchroom or playground duty, straightening up after class, or storing equipment). This habit of trying to reach all students is particularly important in relating to the quiet, submissive, subdued student who can easily be overlooked and ignored.

Another way to interact systematically with students is through written correspondence. Whether the teacher calls the process *journals, letters, notes,* or *insight cards,* encouraging students to write regular messages of some sort to the teacher is helpful. These messages might consist of questions, reactions, arguments, comments, complaints, or suggestions. Their purpose is to open up a system of written communication between the teacher and each student. The teacher can also send brief, written messages to the students by responding to their notes. Teachers who use this system report that some students who rarely speak in class become eloquent when encouraged to present their thoughts in written notes.

The value of systematic patterns of classroom interaction has been documented by Brophy and Evertson (1976). They reported that when teachers call on children to read in a patterned instead of random way, so that children know in advance the order of reading, stress among anxiety-prone students is reduced and excessive competition (a considerable problem among high socioeconomic status children) is lessened.

One further way to reach each student has been suggested by Rosenshine (1970a, 1970b). Among the teaching methods Rosenshine listed as inducing student achievement was a businesslike attitude. Students are more likely to accept invitations to learning when they perceive the teacher as being organized, competent, and prepared for class. This systematic, businesslike approach is especially helpful to the teacher for reaching each student.

Reading Situations

"First of all," he said, "if you can learn a simple trick, Scout, you'll get along a lot better with all kinds of folks. You never really understand a person until you consider things from his point of view — "
"Sir?"
" — until you climb into his skin and walk around in it."
Harper Lee
To Kill a Mockingbird
(1960, p. 36)

To emphasize the importance of reading situations, Aesop tells in one of his fables how the fox is able to cross the thin ice of a pond while other animals, even those who weigh less than the fox, fall through the ice and drown. The fox's secret is that it *listens* to the sound of the ice. Teachers sometimes fail to listen to the sound of students. They react without taking the time to hear what students are saying. Such teacher behavior was described by a junior-high school student who wrote: "My science teacher tries to be a good teacher, but he never listens to anyone. One day I sat next to him in assembly and he asked me how I was doing. I told him that I had a terrible headache. He replied, 'Fine, fine, fine.' He didn't hear a word I said."

Reading situations is the process whereby the teacher attends carefully to students to understand how his or her invitations to learning are being received, interpreted, and acted upon. This general process has been called by various names, including "reflective listening" (Canfield and Wells, 1976), "active listening" (Gordon, 1974), "resonating with the client" (Rogers, 1951), and "attending" (Egan, 1975). Perhaps the blinded Gloucester in Shakespeare's *King Lear* described the process best when he said, "I see it feelingly" (Act IV, Scene vi). But whatever term we use, we are talking about the process teachers use to understand what is occurring within the perceptual world of the student. This calls for *reading behavior backwards*—for looking beyond the student's overt behavior to what that behavior indicates about the student's internal world. A student's bitter complaint of helplessness over an assigned problem, for example, may mean that the student is feeling frustration and is asking for reassurance. This skill of reading behavior backwards is so important that Richards and Richards (1975) postulated that the training of teachers who can understand how things seem from another person's viewpoint should be a major goal of teacher education programs.

In the final analysis, the individual is the world's greatest authority on himself or herself. Only the person with the pain knows where it hurts. For teachers this means that their invitations are invariably perceived by students in the light of the students' past experiences. This has been documented by Dowaliby and Schumer (1973), Felker (1974), and others who have shown that individual students in the classroom each perceive differently what happens to them. To be asked to wash the blackboard may be viewed as most inviting by one child, but as definitely disinviting by another. No two individuals ever share exactly the same past, and no two students ever perceive a teacher's invitation in the same way. If we are to predict the likelihood of an invitation to learning being accepted by a student, we must first have some understanding of how that message might appear and sound in the eyes and ears of the beholder.

Here is an example of how things appear differently when seen from an internal point of view: "Some years ago I had a high-school student who appeared to be very poised and self-confident and who played the guitar with marvelous skill," wrote a teacher. "Yet we could never get him to accept our invitation to perform in public. Other teachers said it was because he felt superior to others in the school. But one day he confided in me that he would dearly love to perform, but stage fright made him physically sick with fear." The skill of listening with care helps teachers to understand the personal world of each student.

Reading situations also enables teachers to see beyond the games students play. Students fear failure much more than most teachers realize. In trying to avoid failure and the resulting embarrassment, students develop entire repertoires of behavior to convince teachers that they are learning when, in fact, they are not. Such repertoires include body stance (leaning forward), eye contact (steady gaze), nonverbal behavior (head nodding), and other activities (note-taking, question-asking, and so on). Students also learn that a successful way to respond when they do not think they can answer a question is to delay, hem and haw, or mumble. Even thinly veiled flattery sometimes misleads teachers into thinking that learning is taking place. That these practices are commonplace is evidenced by research indicating that observer ratings of students' apparent attention fail to correlate with the students' own reports of their attention or with a test of recall (Taylor, 1968).

In simple language, students learn early to pull the wool over teachers' eyes. Many teachers are aware of such ploys. Indeed, they may have used some of them themselves when they were students! Teachers who adopt an inviting approach use a variety of informal, nonthreatening evaluation techniques and discussions to determine what types of invitations to learning may be necessary, and which ones are most likely to be accepted.

Finally, reading situations means that the teacher is alert to the faintest signal from students that might indicate their desire to respond to an invitation: clearing of a throat, leaning forward, hand half-raised, eye contact, or lingering after class. Successful teachers are aware of such positive nonverbal signals and take special responsibility for encouraging acceptance. They also take responsibility for doing everything possible to ensure that students who accept invitations to learning have a good chance of success, for they understand that failure, after taking the risk of accepting an invitation, can have long-lasting negative effects.

A colleague of ours, Mike Fagan, described teacher efforts to maximize chances of student success this way: "An inviting teacher is like a good quarterback in football. When the quarterback throws a pass to a moving receiver, he tries to 'read the situation' and hit the receiver in full stride to maximize his motion, to get into the energy flow of the receiver and to move with him instead of trying to redirect him." By listening for clues in the variations of student behavior, inviting teachers are able to get into the flow of student energy, so chances of misunderstanding are minimized and chances of success are good.

Making Invitations Attractive

Not all invitations are created equal. Dependably inviting teachers are aware of this and use this awareness to design and send messages that have a good chance of being accepted. These messages include body language (smiles, winks, and nods), physical communication (touching that says "I'm glad you're here), and oral communication (statements that convey appreciation and express affirmation). As Grant and Hennings (1971) have documented, factors such as vocal manner, physical space, teacher appearance, and body language all have a significant impact on the communicative process.

Making invitations attractive does not mean that they have to be sugarcoated. Judy Stillion, a colleague, provided this example: "Imagine going to a party where the host offered you a piece of candy, then a jelly doughnut, next a piece of fudge, then a sugar cookie, and finally a cup of sweetened tea to wash it down! This would be hard to stomach." Inviting messages are like delicious and nutritious meals; they provide a variety of tastes and flavors—sweet, bitter, salty, and sour. Too much of one thing, even a good thing, can be disinviting. This applies especially to compliments and praise.

Praise, for example, should be based on honest performance. Praise generally produces increases in effort, but compliments tossed out to students with little or no justification quickly lose all meaning. One student referred to his teacher as a "dead cat teacher": "If you brought her a dead cat, she would praise it." Available research on the counterproductive nature of excessive praise indicates that many young people simply tune out the frequent verbal praise of adults (Brophy and Evertson, 1976), a result probably due to the unrealistic amount of praise distributed by some educators.

The importance of realistic praise has been demonstrated by Rowe (1974c), who found that students ranked "poorest" by teachers actually received more verbal praise than those ranked "best." It was difficult, however, to determine what the bottom students were being praised for; as much as 50 percent of the praise did not appear to be attached to correct responding. Rowe (1974b) commented that bottom students "generally receive an ambiguous signal system" (p. 298). In other words, what these students did or did not do seemed unrelated to the praise they received. By comparison, "top" students received less verbal praise, but the praise they did receive was more pertinent to their responses. What Rowe's research means for teachers is that actions taken to encourage academic achievement and self-regard must be realistic and relevant to honest performance. As an example, the teacher might say, "Bill, you've covered a lot of territory today. You've learned the process of carrying numbers. You should be pleased with your progress." In this way the teacher points to an honest success—one hard to dispute even by the most dispirited student.

Invitations most likely to be accepted and acted upon successfully tend to be appropriate for the situation, are specific enough to be understood, and are not overly demanding. A colleague, Bruce Voelkel, has pointed out that a *limited time* invitation may be especially useful to educators. An example of a limited time invitation would be for a teacher to say to a colleague "I have only ten minutes before I must attend a meeting, but meanwhile, let's go have a cup of coffee." Such an invitation lets the other person know that he or she is not investing a great deal of time and thus makes the invitation easier to accept.

Ensuring Delivery

Invitations are like letters—some get lost in the mail. Unless they are received they do not count. People cannot accept invitations they have never received. Teachers who are dependably inviting check to see that their invitations are received and acknowledged. Their messages are like registered mail; special steps are taken to ensure delivery.

A good way to ensure delivery is through clarity. Clear, direct invitations are far more likely to be recognized and acted upon than vague or indirect ones—just as an invitation asking "Please come for dinner on Saturday evening, October 22, at 8:00 P.M." has a better chance of acceptance than one saying "Let's get together sometime." In addition, a specific invitation makes it easier for students to recognize and acknowledge invitations: "Mark, what did I ask you to do?" If the teacher's invitation is acknowledged but still not accepted, at least the cards are on the table. The teacher is now in a better position to understand the situation. Did nonacceptance mean rejection, or does the student need time to consider? If the invitation was rejected, why? How can it be made acceptable? If it cannot be made acceptable, then what alternate invitations might lead to the same results? By ensuring delivery, the teacher can make many choices apparent.

Checking the receipt of invitations is also important because students sometimes do not know how to respond or cannot respond appropriately, to a teacher's invitations. Often students would like to accept an invitation to learning, but for personal reasons feel unable to do so. Because of self-doubt ("How could I ever learn this stuff?"), threat ("I'm afraid I'll look stupid if I try"), hostility ("They just want to make fun of me"), fear of disappointing others ("I'm not sure I can live up to her expectations"), or resignation ("I *know* I can't do math"), many students have difficulty in responding to even the most attractive invitations. Knowing this, dependably inviting teachers work to make sure that their invitations are received and acknowledged. Ensuring delivery is particularly important when working with certain students.

Students with special problems are likely to perceive the teacher's invitations in unusual ways. What is sent is not always what is received. The same encouragement may have sharply different meanings to different children, even children of the same age. The shy, insecure child may experience great anxiety at a teacher's invitation to read a story in front of the class. A child with high self-assurance may find the same invitation very appealing. Also, children with severe behavioral difficulties, or children filled with feelings of anger and frustration, may find acceptance of the most well-meaning invitations from teachers or peers very difficult. One teacher described such a student this way: "Tracy comes to school each day with hands clenched tightly, face in a frown. Nothing ever seems to go right for him. The least thing a child does to him will definitely end in a fight. His peers are always cheating him when playing games. The teacher has never liked him. The work is too hard. He leaves school each day with hands clenched tightly, face in a frown."

Children like Tracy are likely to hide their true feelings, and a teacher's invitations to feel able, valuable, and responsible may appear to be the last things they want. But inviting teachers are not misled. They understand that students who hold negative feelings about themselves face a great risk when they accept a teacher's invitation because they become vulnerable to further hurt. They also understand that, for students who have been consistently disinvited, a handful of invitations will seldom be enough to make an observable difference in behavior. Inviting teachers recognize the problems involved yet continue to believe their consistent efforts are worthwhile. They recognize the importance of persistence, and so they invite again and again and again, filling the classroom with invitations, then checking that these messages are received, acknowledged, and perhaps acted upon.

Negotiating

The inviting process is a cooperative activity. It involves the participation of both the sender and the receiver. The sender determines the rules under which invitations are sent; the receiver determines the rules of acceptance. These rules are negotiable. For example, the teacher might say, "Mary, I would like you to help me decorate the stage for tomorrow's assembly." Mary replies, "I can't come right now, but I'll come after my conference with Mr. Miller." The negotiation is successfully concluded when the teacher says, "Fine, I'll be looking for you after your conference." Willingness to negotiate is an important part of invitational education.

In seeking acceptance of an invitation a teacher can subtly communicate, "Will you accept? If not now, when? If not this one, which one?" Willingness to negotiate is most important because often students will not accept an invitation when first offered just to see if the teacher really means it. Inviting teachers do not give up easily. They are consistent and dependable in their stance.

Negotiating is not the simple repetition of the same invitation in the same way, over and over, like a broken record. As Walter Barbe commented in a 1977 in-service workshop address at Marshall University: "If you've told a child a thousand times, and the child still has not learned, then it is not the child who is the slow learner." The rejection of an invitation is one indication that the message may benefit by being amended and resubmitted.

Recognizing that an invitation to learning has been rejected, a teacher might confront the student with the question, "If you won't accept this invitation, what invitation will you accept?" The purpose of negotiation is to seek a "doing with" rather than a "doing to" classroom.

Many teachers at various levels have discovered the value of a contract grading system. Students contract for a particular grade to be earned on the basis of the work they help to choose and promise to perform. Another approach might offer the student choices among alternatives that are made an appealing as possible: "You may choose to study vocabulary in small groups or play a word recognition game." This confronts the student with firm expectations within a framework of respect.

Negotiating, as Fisher and Ury (1981) point out, is the process of "getting to yes." This involves having a wide variety of choices available that coincide with the mutual interests of all involved. This most certainly is a "doing with" process. However, even in the best of negotiations there is no guarantee that an invitation will be accepted, no matter how attractively designed or artfully presented. This brings us to the skill of handling rejection.

Handling Rejection

Today the majority of teachers are well trained, enthusiastic, and fired with hopes and ambitions for their students. Most teachers find their careers satisfying. They teach in schools filled with zest for learning and respect for feelings. Other teachers, however, find themselves in less fortunate situations, swamped with assignments that appear to have little relevance to education. These nonteaching responsibilities often include locker checks, hall monitoring, money collecting, record keeping, playground supervision, lunchroom patrol, bus duty, and a host of other assignments. Teachers could more easily accept such duties if these responsibilities were not coupled with overcrowded classes, dilapidated facilities, apparently bored and apathetic colleagues, and, perhaps most painful, disinterested and even hostile students who seem to reject the most well-intentioned invitations and to disinvite the most well-meaning teachers.

Faced with numerous rejections, the teacher can easily become disillusioned, bitter, dejected, and may begin to think: "Why should I continue to invite students? My invitations are not accepted. Besides, they're not listed in our behavioral objectives!" When this thinking takes over, another potentially great teacher joins the ranks of teachers living a professional half-life. This loss of spirit and idealism is a terrible blow to education as well as a major calamity for the teacher. Such tragedies need not happen. When teachers operate with patience and courage, conserving and focusing limited energies at the most effective times, they will not be easily intimidated and overwhelmed by apparently impossible situations in which their finest invitations are apparently rejected.

It is essential, first, for teachers to consider whether or not their invitations have *in fact,* been rejected by students. As we have seen, nonacceptance is not the same as rejection. And even an apparent rejection of an invitation is often just the opposite. For example, one beginning teacher invited a student to help him move some supplies after class. "Are you jiving?" the student responded. "I got more important things to do." The teacher was hurt and resentful because he assumed that his invitation had been rudely rejected. Later, he was startled when the student showed up to help. Students accept or reject invitations in their own ways and on their own terms. It is important to understand that acceptances come in many forms. The person extending an invitation determines what is presented, and how, but the person receiving the invitation determines how it will be acted upon, and when.

Even when an invitation is definitely, unmistakenly rejected, it is useful to separate the invitation from the self. Just because a student rejects an invitation does not mean that the student is rejecting the teacher. Students, like all of us, are not so much against others as for themselves. This endless quest for self-esteem was reviewed in Chapter 2. Because of the nature of self-concept, students may reject, accept, or place on hold invitations for countless reasons that have nothing to do with the teacher.

One of the most common reasons for rejection of an invitation is the memory of similar invitations accepted in the past but found less than satisfying. If past invitations have resulted in embarrassment or humiliation, it is a special risk to accept present ones. Teachers who understand this process are less likely to blame themselves or consider it a personal insult when their invitations are rejected. These teachers head back to the drawing board to develop fresh invitations. They are not dismayed—and they are not resigned.

Beyond the psychological reasons for the rejections of invitations, there are also environmental reasons. The physical conditions of room assignment, facilities, lighting, public address system, class size, temperature, general aesthetics, scheduling, even the class makeup of students with varying backgrounds and levels of achievement—all these contribute to the acceptance or rejection of invitations.

For those of us in teaching this means working to avoid taking the rejection of an invitation too personally. Students took a long time to arrive at where they are today, and they will also require time to change. Nevertheless, it is important to remember that everything makes a difference. Any invitation, no matter how small or in what area, has tremendous potential. What appears to be a trifle can, in the right situation, make a significant difference. Teachers have an excellent chance of making a significant difference when they behave trustingly, reach each student, read situations, create attractive invitations, ensure delivery, and are willing to negotiate. Even doing all of these things will not guarantee that an invitation will be accepted. The only sure way to avoid rejection is not to send invitations. But who wants to be an uninviting teacher in an uninviting school?

Following Through

After an invitation is extended, received, and acknowledged, it can be accepted, rejected, negotiated, or put on hold. But the process does not end there; the interaction does not conclude on the student's side of the net. The final moves are made by the teacher who takes responsibility for following through on accepted invitations or analyzing and renegotiating unaccepted ones, and for adding new ones.

Being inviting, as we have seen, provides a way of coming together for some worthwhile purpose. Following through begins with the teacher asking himself or herself: "Were they with me? Were we able to come together, even for a brief time, in some mutually beneficial way?" If the teacher answers yes, the feeling should be a peak educative experience—one of those moments that make teaching so exciting. These moments are to be savored and then stored away, to be brought out when we may be feeling a bit low about our teaching.

On the other hand, if the inviting transaction was less than successful the teacher needs to examine what happened. For example, was the invitation unclear, did the student need more time to consider, did it require too great a commitment of time or energy, did the student lack the skills to be successful, or were there other factors that made the invitation unacceptable? Reflecting on what happened is an important way to increase the probability of future success.

Summary

In this chapter we have seen that being dependably inviting requires energy, sensitivity, intelligence, and imagination. It is a complicated process of decoding obscure messages, reaching for complicated meanings, making unusual connections, and recognizing subtle but significant nuances of human interaction. This is no easy task. However, before we become too overwhelmed, we should tell ourselves that the inviting process is more a journey than a destination. No one ever reaches his or her full potential, yet development is possible and growth can be enjoyable. In Chapter 5 we look at the person in the process. We consider how educators can be more inviting, both personally and professionally, to *themselves* as well as others.

Chapter Five

THE PERSON IN THE PROCESS

In giving attention to the development of a logicalistic methodology for teaching and learning, we may overlook the person who is to teach and the person who is to learn.

Edward C. Weir
"The Meaning of Learning and the Learning of Meaning"
Phi Delta Kappan
(1965, p. 280)

A major goal of invitational education is assisting teachers to become beneficial presences in the lives of others. As explained earlier, this requires a certain perceptual orientation, a particular stance, and a consistency in behavior. This chapter looks at the person in the process and considers what is necessary to sustain the desire and energy to function at an intentionally inviting level—to develop the stamina and courage of the "long-distance" inviter.

Being professionally inviting with others cannot be maintained if it is seen as an isolated series of behaviors a teacher performs when he or she comes to school. As our colleague Charlotte Lambeth pointed out, "Invitational education is only one aspect of invitational living." The person in the process is most important. Therefore, it is important for the inviting professional to develop and orchestrate the following four areas, first identified by a founder and continuing contributor to invitational education, Betty Siegel.

Being personally inviting with oneself

Being personally inviting with others

Being professionally inviting with oneself

Being professionally inviting with others

The dependably inviting teacher is one who can balance and orchestrate the demands of these areas, thereby facilitating optimal personal and professional development in oneself and others. Let us examine these four areas in turn, and introduce some ways to increase one's "IQ" (Invitational Quotient).

Being Personally Inviting with Oneself

Many people go throughout life committing partial suicide—destroying their talents, energies, creative qualities. Indeed, to learn how to be good to oneself is often more difficult than to learn how to be good to others.

Joshua Liebman
Peace of Mind
(1946, p. 46)

There are countless teachers who are dedicated, caring, and hardworking but who are experiencing chronic discouragement, dejection, and frustration. These feelings are summed up in the single word *burnout,* defined by Edelwich (1980) as the "progressive loss of idealism, energy and purpose" (p. 14). Sometimes burnout is self-inflicted.

When professionals constantly sacrifice their own wants and needs to meet the demands of others, the sacrifice gradually builds resentment. As one teacher put it, "Teachers have a moral obligation to their students to take care of themselves." This opinion is supported by Knowles (1977), who points out that although over 99 percent of us are born healthy, many of us later become ill as a result of personal misbehavior and self-abuse. Knowles believes that we have "a public duty" to preserve our own health. Thus, if one aspires to go the distance, to be a long-distance inviter, it is vital to view oneself and one's potential positively, and to invite oneself to realize this potential.

Being personally inviting with oneself is a tremendously important enterprise for teachers. As an old Virginia mountaineer commented, "You can't come back from somewhere you ain't been." It is difficult to invite others if we neglect to invite ourselves. Coudert (1965) stated:

> The single relationship truly central and crucial in a life is the relationship to the self. It is rewarding to find someone whom you like, but it is essential to like yourself. It is quickening to recognize that someone is a good and decent human being, but it is indispensable to view yourself as acceptable. It is a delight to discover people who are worthy of admiration and respect and love, but it is vital to believe yourself deserving of these things. (p. 118)

If we believe that invitations are important, then we should apply this belief to our own lives—to stand tall, dress well, eat less, take exercise, become involved, and find ways to be fully *present* in this world.

In being personally inviting with oneself, it is helpful to keep in mind that the principles most useful for inviting others also directly apply to inviting oneself. The most important principle is respect for oneself and one's feelings. For example, if exercising at night after a hard day of teaching feels terribly difficult, the teacher might try a self-invitation to exercise in the morning. If this doesn't work, a self-invitation to play a sport, join a health club, buy an exercise bicycle or minitrampoline, or take a long walk each evening might accomplish the same thing. The goal is to send self-invitations that are most likely to be accepted and acted upon. By listening to our own feelings and varying our self-invitations we increase the probability of success.

Following are some examples of ways to maintain one's own personal energy level and nurture oneself physically, emotionally, and spiritually, although it is beyond the scope of this book to go into detail about being personally inviting with oneself.

Take pleasure in stillness   Too much isolation can be bad, but taking time to be alone is helpful. Enjoy silence. Contemplate and meditate on who you are, where you came from, and where you're going. Being at one with yourself can be deeply rewarding.

Keep in reasonable shape   Maintain physical health. Whether you choose an individual effort (long walks, jogging, exercising, gardening) or an organized sport (bowling, tennis, racketball), it is important to maintain the body in which you live.

Plan a long life   Take personal responsibility for your own life support system. Be choosy about what and how much you eat. Eliminate cigarettes and other injurious substances. Maintain health care, and fasten your safety belt!

Give yourself a celebration   Make a pledge to do something special for just yourself in the immediate future. It might be a bubble bath, a fishing expedition, a good novel, a shopping trip, a new outfit, a favorite meal, a round of golf, attending a film or play; celebrate!

Recharge your batteries   Handle short-term burnout by talking things over with a friend whom you consider to have good sense. Just talking about concerns helps to avoid accepting a lot of guilt and anxiety. A good friend can help you find ways to invite yourself.

Live with a flourish   Find satisfaction from many sources, such as a hobby or activity unrelated to your professional life. As much as realistically possible, surround yourself with things you like. Laugh a little. Take a few risks, travel, and assert yourself. The goal is to avoid drabness and live with a flourish.

These suggestions can help prevent "burning the teacher at both ends."

One additional way teachers might invite themselves personally is by taking time to remember what it was like to be a child and letting their own feelings find expression. The death of a child is tragic, so why kill the child in ourselves? We keep our zest for living alive by trusting our feelings, by being open to experience, by being gentle with ourselves, and, when necessary, forgiving ourselves. After all, errors are primarily sources of information.

Inviting ourselves is facilitated when we are personally inviting with others; let us turn our attention to how we can make this take place.

Being Personally Inviting with Others

The second important area in becoming a long-distance inviter is being *personally* inviting with others. In most human interactions there is a basic process of interdependence: the greatest life support systems are relatives and friends, and invitational education places a high priority on personal relationships. Professional success, no matter how great, cannot make up for lack of success in personal relationships. It is important to cultivate and treasure a circle of trusted friends and acquaintances as well as to seek out new relationships and explore fresh interests.

A most important aspect of inviting others personally is being "real." Carl Rogers (1965, 1967, 1976) and Sidney Jourard (1964, 1968), among others, have emphasized the importance of appropriate self-disclosure in interpersonal relationships. Disclosure begets disclosure, and it often helps to share personal feelings, to acknowledge that we all wake up on the wrong side of bed, go in the wrong bathroom, and forget appointments—to be able to invite others to know us as we really are.

One additional aspect of inviting others personally is to develop and maintain unconditional regard and respect for other human beings. As discussed earlier, comments or behaviors that are perceived by others as demeaning or insulting are usually perceived as disinviting regardless of one's intentions. Kidding others about their physical appearance, behavior, background, or misfortunes can often be very disinviting. Saying "I was only kidding" may not be sufficient to repair the damage of a cruel jest. As someone wrote: "Sticks and stones may break my bones, but words will surely kill me." Here are some practical ways to avoid lethal statements and to be personally inviting with others:

Promote civility   Common courtesy is a most important tool of the inviting teacher. This is usually accomplished by greeting others by name, showing respect by being prompt with appointments and commitments, promoting "please" and "thank you," and in general showing basic concern and appreciation for others and their feelings.

Let people know you care   Often we send a get well card to those who are ill but forget to send a welcome back note as well. A thoughtful birthday, holiday, congratulatory, or other card or note to relatives, colleagues, students, and friends lets them know that they are in your thoughts.

Warm up the class   At the beginning of each class period a personal greeting, a little light humor, a brief comment on world events, an inquiry into how things are going, can set the stage for learning. Just as joggers should limber up their muscles before jogging, teachers should limber up their classes before teaching.

Break bread together   One of the oldest forms of community is sharing a bit of food and drink. By arranging for something during break or other appropriate times, the stage is set for the facilitation of good feelings and friendships.

Keep things simple   When someone comes with a complaint, avoid second-level problems, such as an angry exchange or countercomplaints. Focus on what the person is saying, listen carefully, and be willing to express regret (this is not the same as an apology). If possible, take some positive action to let the person know that at least you listened and understood his or her feelings.

Stay abreast   Make a special effort to enter the world in which the student of today lives. Keep abreast of contemporary fads, fashions, heroes, films, sports, actors, singers, and other current student interests. Using an example from real life can be both personally and professionally inviting.

Positive beliefs about people coupled with a dependable stance and personally inviting behaviors are basic to invitational education. Yet, as important as it is to be *personally* inviting with yourself and others, it takes even more effort and skill to become *professionally* inviting. This brings us to the next two areas—being professionally inviting with oneself and being professionally inviting with others.

Being Professionally Inviting with Oneself

It is difficult to overestimate the importance of being active in one's own professional development. The teacher who does not invite himself or herself to grow professionally runs the risk of becoming obsolete and living an intellectual half-life. Therefore, it is vital that teachers continue to be actively engaged in upgrading their skills and knowledge and finding ways to sustain their professional enthusiasm.

There are many ways for teachers to grow professionally. An especially challenging one is to develop a model of teaching (Joyce and Weil, 1980). Sometimes teachers get locked into a certain style of teaching, especially if they have experienced some success with it. Being in a rut, even a successful one, narrows perspective and diminishes professional vitality. The following list represents suggestions for discovering new approaches to being professionally inviting with yourself.

Participate in programs   In addition to typical academic courses, programs, and degrees, there are special conferences and workshops that can provide exciting ways to sharpen skills, learn techniques, and develop new understandings. Attending such professional activities will help upgrade skills and knowledge.

Spend time reading   There are countless professional books, journals, magazine articles, newsletters, monographs, and the like that are expressly written to help teachers develop professionally. Finding some time each day to read is an excellent way to stay abreast.

Join professional groups   Be active in professional societies. Working within these organizations to ensure that they maintain high professional quality is important in strengthening yourself professionally.

Conduct projects Some teachers might assume that research should be left to scientists in laboratories, surrounded by computers and data sheets. But bigger is not necessarily better. A teacher's quiet investigation of some question can have a long-range influence.

Write papers A valuable way to invite yourself professionally is to write for professional publications. Not everything written must appear in national journals. There are numerous local, state, and regional newsletters, journals, and related publications that welcome contributions from educators in the field.

Arrange a date Are there people in your professional world who you admire and would like to know better? If so, be brave! Invite them to lunch. If you invite, they may accept. If you don't, they can't.

Seek feedback At the end of each semester seek suggestions from students. Find out how they evaluate your teaching and what you might do to make it better. This way you can be showing respect for the opinions of students while strengthening yourself professionally.

Personal and professional growth ultimately culminates in being better able to be professionally inviting with others.

Being Professionally Inviting with Others

The primary purpose of education, as we view the process, is to invite people to realize their potential, to meet the needs of society, and to participate in the progress of civilization. This is best accomplished by building on the three areas we have already considered. When these three areas are functioning at an optimal level, the stage is set for being professionally inviting with others.

Because the process of being professionally inviting with others is the central focus of this book, it is necessary to go into greater detail in this area than in the previous three. Let us begin our examination of the fourth area by using self-concept as a springboard.

Earlier we reviewed evidence indicating a significant relationship between self-concept and school achievement. On the basis of this evidence, we can see that students' perceptions of themselves as learners apparently serve as personal guidance systems to direct their classroom behavior. Because the self-concepts of students as learners play a critical part in their academic performance, a professional understanding of self-concept theory, coupled with skills for interpreting how students view themselves as learners, are important tools.

Ways to be professionally inviting with others are suggested by research provided by the Florida Key (Purkey, Cage, and Graves, 1973), an inventory of student behaviors designed to infer students' self-concepts as learners. The Key has been used since 1972 to investigate various groups of students, to compare disadvantaged and nondisadvantaged pupils (Owen, 1972), to analyze professed and inferred self-concepts of students (Graves, 1972) and to study students identified as disruptive and nondisruptive (Branch, 1974).

In making deductions about self-concept, most researchers have focused on global self-concepts rather than on situation-specific self-images, such as self as athlete, self as family member, self as learner, or self as friend. By observing only global self-concept—which is many-faceted and contains diverse, even conflicting, subselves—investigators have sometimes overlooked the importance of these subsystems. In comparison, the Key research limited itself to the situation-specific self-concept that seems to relate most closely to school success or failure: self as learner.

Four factors that relate significantly to school performance were derived through factor analysis in the Key research. These factors were labeled (1) relating, (2) asserting, (3) investing, and (4) coping. Examination of these four factors is useful, for they suggest ways in which teachers may be professionally inviting with others.

Relating

The highest expression of civilization is not its art but the supreme tenderness that people are strong enough to feel and show toward one another.

Norman Cousins
Editoral in Saturday Review
(January 23, 1971, p. 31)

The quality identified on the Key as having the greatest significance to the concept of the self as learner is *relating*. As measured by the Key, the relating score indicates the level of trust and appreciation that the student maintains toward others.

Students who score high in relating identify closely with classmates, teachers, and school. They express positive feelings about learning and they think in terms of *our* school, *our* teachers, and *my* classmates (as opposed to *the* teacher, *that* school, or *those* kids). Getting along with others is easy for those who score high on relating and are thus able to take a natural, relaxed approach to school life. They are likely to stay calm when things go wrong, and they can express feelings of frustration or impatience without exploding.

Students who score low on relating seem unable to involve themselves in school activities or with teachers and other students. One teacher depicted such a student as follows:

> Two summers ago, I tutored children who were having
> problems learning to read. Looking back, I can see how their
> reading problems were related to how they saw themselves.
> One boy, John, who was ten years old, was not well liked
> because of his habit of criticizing others to make himself feel
> important. His poor self-concept and failure to relate to others
> were graphically illustrated one day when a huge whipped
> cream fight was held on an empty hilltop. Whipped cream
> filled the air for twenty minutes or so as forty kids, each with
> two or three cans, went wild. After the cream had settled, and
> later that day, John told me he had to spray whipped cream
> on himself as no one else made a point of doing so.

To be ignored, even in a whipped cream battle, can be a most painful experience.

To be overlooked or ignored by their peers is an intolerable situation for most students, and they will go to great lengths to gain acceptance. When the desire for positive human relationships is unfulfilled in conventional ways, students are likely to try less conventional or socially unacceptable ways. For example, according to Cartwright, Tomson, and Schwartz (1975) and others, the potential delinquent joins a gang to gain a feeling of status denied by the larger society.

The following passage from *Manchild in the Promised Land* by Claude Brown (1965) illustrates the pathetic efforts of one young girl to buy human relationships:

> I found out that Sugar would bring candy and pickles to class
> and give them to Carole, so Carole liked her and wanted me
> to like her too. After I got used to Sugar being ugly and
> having buckteeth, I didn't mind her always hanging around,
> and I stopped beating her up. Sugar started coming around on
> the weekends, and she always had money and wanted to take
> me to the show. Sometimes I would go with Sugar, and
> sometimes I would just take her money and go with
> somebody else. Most of the time I would take Sugar's money
> then find Bucky and take him to the show. Sugar used to cry,
> but I don't think she really minded it too much, because she
> knew she was ugly and had to have something to give people
> if she wanted them to like her. I never could get rid of Sugar.
> She would follow me around all day long and would keep
> trying to give me things, and when I didn't take them, she
> would start looking real pitiful and say she didn't want me to
> have it anyway. The only way I could be nice to Sugar was to
> take everything she had, so I started being real nice to her. (p. 55)

From literary descriptions as well as scientific research, it is clear that peer relationships have significant influence on self-concept and school achievement (Damico, 1974, 1976).

Forcing students to relate to each other in positive and productive ways is undesirable and probably impossible, but teachers can create an inviting atmosphere in which relating is facilitated. A specific teacher behavior that invites feelings of belonging in students is the use of "we" statements to suggest groups membership, encouraging students to involve themselves in school activities that become *our* curriculum, *our* decorations, *our* rules, *our* efforts to keep things clean. Instructional programs can be developed and presented in ways that encourage students to play a cooperative part. For example, Leviton and Kiraly (1979) have shown that using students as tutors is a good way to accomplish cooperation. Relating is also encouraged by the teacher's use of students' names at every opportunity. Reis (1972) has provided a series of techniques for teachers who have a hard time remembering names.

Finally, creation of the proper atmosphere for relating involves the removal of barriers. Particular skill is necessary, as Haskins and Butts (1973) stress, to avoid a mismatch between the communication system of the classroom and that of the minority-group student. As we have seen, teachers may be unintentionally disinviting when they appear to be condescending, patronizing, or over-friendly. "That English teacher tries to be helpful," a student commented, "but she always talks about how 'you blacks can be proud of what you've done.' It shows me that she is constantly aware of the differences and thinks in terms of labels." Teachers who want to be professionally inviting with others work to avoid labels, expressions, and actions likely to be offensive to minority-group members. This requires sensitivity to how things seem from the other person's point of view.

The way one faculty advisor helped remove barriers to relating is described by Combs et al. (1978). A group of students and their advisor were trying to decide how to spend the money in their club treasury (this episode occurred during the Great Depression of the 1930s when money was scarce):

> Somebody suggested giving a party for the school. Another said, "Well, it ought to be for everybody." The advisor said, "Let's see if we can figure out a way of getting everybody into the act." Someone else suggested "Well, we could have a dance. But if we have a dance, the people who can't dance won't come." Then another person said, "Well, maybe we could have a dance that everybody will come to." That was a novel idea and the question immediately arose as to what kind of dance it could be. Somebody came up with the idea, "Let's have a square dance, and we will teach them when they get there." Since this was a large city high school and nobody knew how to square dance, so far as anyone knew, this met the criterion.
>
> Then somebody said, "Even if we have a square dance, some people won't come because they don't have the right clothes." The reply: "Well, this is a country dance; we won't let

anyone in who looks too sharp!" And that was adopted as policy. Somebody else pointed out, "Well, they won't come if they aren't able to get a date," and somebody else countered, "We could make it stag. We could let the boys in one door and let the girls in the other on opposite sides of the gym, and nobody would know who had a date."

Then somebody suggested: "Some people won't come because they won't have enough money and after the dance was over they would want to buy something to eat for the girl they were with." So it was decided, "Let's feed them at the dance." A committee was set up to enlist the aid of mothers in baking cakes and another to make a deal with a soft drink distributor. After all this, someone said, "We've still got a problem: Some won't come because they can't afford it." After much figuring on the cost of the band and an estimate of how many people would come, the price of the dance was finally set at eight cents. Many people had doubts whether such a program would succeed and said, "It will never work!" When the night of the dance finally came, the largest crowd turned out that had ever been in the gymnasium. In fact, so many people came that nobody could dance! (pp. 151–52)

The ways in which individuals relate to a group correlate highly with how much the individuals feel the group likes and respects them (Tagiuri, Bruner, and Blake, 1958). Teachers who understand the importance of relating work to remove barriers and encourage positive relationships in the classroom.

Asserting

That which gave me most Uneasiness among those Maids of Honour, when my Nurse carried me to visit them, was to see them use me without any Matter of Ceremony, like a Creature who had no Sort of Consequence.

Jonathan Swift
Gulliver's Travels
(1961, p. 95)

The second factor identified in the Key research, *asserting,* describes another aspect of self-concept as learner—the one that characterizes students' sense of control over what happens to them in the classroom. Students who score high on the asserting factor speak up for their own ideas and are not afraid to ask questions in class. They actively participate in school activities and talk to others about their academic interests.

The importance of asserting oneself has been stressed by Alberti and Emmons (1974), who define assertive behavior as those personal actions that enable one to act in one's own best interests, to stand up for oneself without undue anxiety, to express one's honest feelings comfortably, and to exercise one's own rights without denying the rights of others. Alberti and Emmons view assertive behavior as the affirming of one's own rights (in contrast to aggressive behavior, which is directed against others) and the "perfect right" of every individual in interpersonal relationships. Beyond affirming one's own rights, assertive behavior also involves the ability to express feelings of positive regard, appreciation, and love—to let others know their presence invites a celebration.

Advantages of assertive behavior have been documented by a number of researchers (Cotler and Guerra, 1976; Seligman, 1975). Seligman, who has formulated a theory of learned helplessness, states that the experience of internal control is essential to both positive self-esteem and good psychological health; negative self-regard and psychological depression are the likely results of feelings of helplessness. The problem with learned helplessness is that when one learns to believe that one lacks control, this belief persists even when circumstances have altered so that it does become possible to assert oneself (Lefcourt, 1976; Phares, 1976). This finding supports Coleman's research (1966), which reported that one's feelings of control over what happens to oneself as a student are strongly related to school success.

Assertive behavior can be learned, as Alberti and Emmons (1974) have demonstrated, and can therefore be taught by teachers who invite dialogue and expression of different viewpoints in the classroom and who maintain a respect for the right of students to express these viewpoints. Class activities such as values-clarification or moral reasoning exercises have been strongly advocated by Bennett and Novak (1981), Kohlberg (1969), Kohlberg and Turiel (1971), Simon, Howe, and Kirschenbaum (1978), and others. Many teachers have used such activities to encourage students to explore their own values.

Teachers can also encourage assertive behavior in their students by teaching them how to express themselves in socially acceptable ways without aggressing against others or denying others' rights. Some children learn to assert themselves early, as evidenced by the words of a little girl, overheard on a playground: "Just because I don't know how to jump doesn't mean that I always have to turn the rope!" Significant differences exist between the assertion of rights and aggression against others. Both teachers and students benefit when they understand these differences and employ assertion rather than aggression in interpersonal relationships.

An additional advantage of inviting students to assert themselves has been described by Gaudry and Spielberger (1971), who investigated relationships between student anxiety and school achievement. As might be expected, they found that anxiety-prone students harbor strong self-derogatory attitudes. Because highly anxious students doubt themselves and their abilities and have a difficult time in asserting themselves, they become vulnerable to future failure. "I'll never be any good in math," a student wrote. "One time I was borrowing and I got the *whole* paper of twenty problems wrong!"

Significant to our discussion, Gaudry and Speilberger found that high-anxiety students actually improved their examination performance when they were invited to assert themselves by writing comments on the test items. By expressing why they selected a particular answer, students seemed to feel less anxious about their work. When students are invited to assert themselves in socially acceptable ways, their feelings about themselves and their abilities are likely to improve along with their academic performance.

A further way to encourage student assertion is to teach them how to avoid or bypass roadblocks to learning. A big problem for many students, especially those who are highly anxious, is what to do when they do not know the correct answer. In oral reading, a student who does not know a word will usually stammer, stutter, and suffer painful pauses until the teacher or another student supplies the answer. Much of this effort is counterproductive and can sometimes be avoided if the teacher invites students to jump over the difficult problem and keep going. In oral reading, for example, the student can bypass the unknown word by replacing it with the words *hard word* and keep going. In a multiple choice test, the student can be told to select an option and move on. The important thing for a student is not to get blocked or hung up on an endless regression that often leads to lowered performance and self-esteem.

One final method useful in inviting students to assert themselves is to show them that going from something to something is much easier than going from nothing to something. By getting started, even if the start is poor, students begin their journey toward improvement and excellence. Contrary to the standard advice that "if it's worth doing, it's worth doing well," encouraging students to do things poorly, at least in the beginning, may be helpful. Doing things well results from first doing things poorly.

Investing

No Columbus, no Marco Polo has ever seen stranger and more fascinating and thoroughly absorbing sights than the child that learns to perceive, to taste, to smell, to touch, to hear and see, and to use his body, his senses, and his mind. No wonder that the child shows an insatiable curiosity. He has the whole world to discover. Education and learning, while on the one hand furthering this process of discovery, on the other hand gradually broke and finally stopped it completely. There are relatively few adults who are fortunate enough to have retained something of the child's curiosity, his capacity for questioning and for wondering.

Ernest G. Schachtel
Metamorphosis: On the Development of Affect,
Perception, Attention, and Memory
(1959, p. 292)

The third factor identified by the Key research is the creative part of self-concept as learner: *investing*. This factor encompasses student willingness to speculate, guess, and try new things. Students who score high in investing seek out things to do in school without the prompting of extrinsic rewards such as tokens, gold stars, grades, points, or praise. Their reward appears to be the activity itself.

Many researchers have suggested the importance of investing behavior. Goldberg (1960) reviewed the results of a study, sponsored by the Talented Youth Project of the Horace Mann–Lincoln Institute, that examined underachievement among academically talented students. He found that although underachievers perceived themselves as "less able to learn" and "less confident," their level of aspiration remained high. Many students would apparently like to accept teacher invitations, but because of self-doubt have a difficult time investing themselves. Teachers can encourage students to invest themselves in learning by posing open-ended questions and by using wait-time. Let us examine these two techniques more closely.

Open-ended questions do more than require students to regurgitate known facts. They are varied and interesting and ask students to interpret meanings, give opinions, compare and contrast ideas, or combine facts to form general principles. Here are a few examples: What would it be like if we were all born with only two fingers on each hand? What if the South had won the Civil War? What if the earth's axis shifted five degrees? What if the supply of oil were exhausted? What if a license were required to have a child? What if the world became a one-party democracy? Or, even more simply, "What is justice?" "Loyalty?" "Happiness?" "Truth?" Such questions can stir student imagination, create excitement in the classroom, and encourage all students to invest themselves in the discussions. (As one student wrote about her teacher: "She would ask us questions that really made us think!") George Kelly (1963) emphasized the value of questions this way:

> I suspect that historically the questions men have asked have
> turned out to be more important than the conclusions they
> reached. Questions breed actions that lead to further
> questions, and these, in turn, to the boldness of further
> inquiring acts. Conclusions, however, perpetuate themselves
> and often serve to limit, if not stultify, both action and
> thought. Thus, the living history of man is the story of the
> questions he has enacted, rather than the conclusions he has
> anchored in science or dogma. (p. 12)

Asking provocative, open-ended questions is an excellent way to invite student investment in learning, particularly when the questions are followed by sufficient wait-time.

Wait-time is the time allowed for a student's response to a teacher's question, or the time given to a student for elaboration after initial response to a question. In her research on wait-time, Rowe (1974a, 1974b, 1974c) demonstrated that silence can be more inviting than words. She reported that speech, when uninterrupted, tends to come in bursts separated by intervals of silence, particularly when students are attempting to answer a difficult question. By analyzing recordings of classroom interactions, Rowe found that the average wait-time of teachers was about one second. If an answer was not forthcoming within that second, teachers tended to repeat or rephrase the question, ask a different question, or call on another student. Furthermore, when a student did make an initial response, teachers tended to react within one second with praise, an additional question, or some other interjection. By reacting immediately (within one second) to the student's initial burst, the teacher cut off the student's efforts to answer and elaborate.

Rowe's research indicates that when teachers increase their wait-time from the usual one second to three to five seconds, the length of student responses increases, the number of unsolicited, but appropriate, responses increases, and failure to respond decreases. Therefore, a good way to invite students to invest themselves in classroom happenings is to give them sufficient wait-time.

A second important aspect of Rowe's research is her documentation of the differential treatment teachers give to students. When teachers were asked to designate the "five best" and "five poorest" students in their classes, Rowe found that the amount of wait-time allowed each group was not the same. The "five-best" received nearly two seconds to begin an answer, while the "five poorest" received slightly less than one second. Findings that low-achieving students receive less wait-time have also been reported by Brophy and Good (1974) and Campbell (1973). For teachers this means that a most productive way to encourage students' investments in learning is to ask open-ended questions and then to be sure that each student has equal wait-time in which to respond and elaborate. As Jerome Bruner (1960) has pointed out, "The shrewd guess, the fertile hypothesis, the courageous leap to a tentative conclusion—these are the most valuable coin of the thinker at work" (p. 14). Dependably inviting teachers use a variety of methods to encourage investing. Some of these techniques are presented in Appendix A.

Coping

Be a good loser as you learned in school.
The Wing Commander
Screenplay by Seton I. Miller and Dan Totheroh
Dawn Patrol
(Warner Brothers, 1930)

Coping, the fourth and final factor identified by the Key research, indicates how well students seem to be meeting school requirements.

Students who score high in this area apparently possess an image of themselves as able and willing to meet school expectations. They believe in their own academic ability and take pride in their classroom performance. They usually pay attention in class, do their work with care, finish what they start, and expect success from their efforts. Students who score high in coping have discovered and use an important tool of learning: reading. They often pursue reading independently, even when it sometimes interferes with other school activities.

Coping is another name for school success, a subject emphasized throughout this book. What has not been sufficiently emphasized so far is that no single factor is more relevant to feelings of coping than the act of coping itself. By successfully coping with school expectations, students develop a sense of competence. "I know I can spell," an elementary school student wrote. "I got a good note one time." This sense of competence is a significant part of positive self-regard.

The feeling of competence gained through doing something that works is particularly valuable for children in the elementary grades. When children are successful at leading a class activity, giving a weather report, passing out material, collecting milk money, taking the roll, delivering a note, or storing playground equipment, they are using learned skills to do things that work. Things that work in higher grades include planning and preparing a complete dinner in home economics, plotting a lot of land in math class, changing spark plugs in auto repair class, reading a French menu in a foreign language class, or executing a double reverse in football. One student described the process of learning something that works as follows: "My first two years at school I was terrible at physical education. 'Any girl can kick better than you,' I was told. I was always picked last for kickball teams because I could not kick the ball into the air (a firm rule was *no grounders*). On one particular day in third grade, my teacher, who was sitting with another teacher watching the game, saw that I was soon about to take my turn and undoubtedly kick grounders until I was out. This lady (all six feet of her) called me aside and showed me how to kick *under* the ball. When I got up to kick, the ball sailed in the air! I'll always remember that teacher who took the time to show me that I could do something that works!" Any honest success experience, no matter how small or in what area, helps students discover that they can cope.

There are times, of course, when students are not coping and it is necessary to point out their errors. But teachers should not view this as an inconsequential act. Pointing out mistakes, as Dewey believed, "should not wither the sources of creative insight. Before individuals can produce significant things, they must first produce" (cited in Hook, 1939, p. 19). As Elkind (1981) has indicated, the stress from fear of failure makes it difficult for children to take the risk of learning. In the classroom, this means that to do things well, students must first do. Dependably inviting teachers recognize that experience emerges from inexperience, and that learning is a process of trying things out, of finding what works and what does not.

Rather than focusing on mistakes and criticizing poor performance, teachers who are dependably inviting encourage students to feel confident in coping with errors and overcoming them. One high-school girl told how this was accomplished for her: "I was being auditioned for a part in our high-school musical. I was very nervous and worried about getting the part. At the end of my song my voice cracked and I thought my acting and singing days were over. The director looked at me and smiled, saying 'Let's just hope you hit that note on opening night.' It was definitely the warmest feeling I've ever experienced." When students understand that making mistakes is normal, expected, and understandable, they are in a good position to develop positive, realistic self-concepts as learners.

The four factors of the Florida Key—relating, asserting, investing, and coping—can serve to identify techniques that teachers may use to invite students to develop positive self-concepts as learners as well as to encourage academic achievement.

We've seen that the inviting process involves the orchestration of four basic areas: (1) being personally inviting with oneself, (2) being personally inviting with others, (3) being professionally inviting with oneself, and (4) being professionally inviting with others. The successful educator is one who can balance the demands of the four areas and integrate them into a smooth pattern of functioning, thereby facilitating personal and professional development in himself or herself and in others.

Concentrating too much effort in only one or two of the four areas creates an imbalance. Teachers who are only personally inviting with themselves run the risk of being self-centered participants in what Lasch (1979) named the "culture of narcissism." These teachers care little about others, and others care little about them. Teachers who overemphasize the second area, who have an obsession with being personally inviting with others, may find that they are well liked but that they are not good teachers. Teachers who are obsessed with being professionally inviting with themselves alone may find excessive isolation, having a great deal to say but no one to listen. Finally, teachers who are professionally inviting with others at the expense of the other three areas are likely to find themselves burning out. When any of the four areas of functioning is neglected, all areas suffer. The ideal teacher, from an invitational education viewpoint, is one who orchestrates all four areas of functioning, taking care to develop equally in each area.

Summary

Chapter 5 has highlighted the importance of the person in the invitational process. Four basic areas of functioning were presented: being personally inviting with oneself, being personally inviting with others, being professionally inviting with oneself, and being professionally inviting with others. Each of these areas was seen as equally important. The successful educator is one who artfully blends and synchronizes the four areas and is thus able to sustain the energy and enthusiasm of the long-distance inviter. Our final chapter offers an *inviting family* model for the schools of tomorrow, and compares it with that of an *efficient factory.*

Chapter Six

TWO MODELS FOR TOMORROW'S SCHOOLS

All education springs from some image of the future.

Alvin Toffler
Learning for Tomorrow
(1974, p. 32)

Just as students possess relatively untapped potential for development, educators possess relatively untapped potential for encouraging this
development. So far this book has emphasized what the individual educator can do. This emphasis is important because teachers, administration,
and staff have the power to promote human potential—even in the face of
bureaucratic policies, apathetic colleagues, inadequate facilities, and
poorly designed programs. The educator facing such negative forces can
still be a profoundly beneficial presence in the lives of others. Of course,
inviting success is much more enjoyable and is more likely to occur when
everybody and everything in and around schools are working together to
accomplish this goal.

It is not the purpose of this book to examine in detail administrative
policies, instructional programs, or physical plants. Yet clear evidence
exists, as presented by Brubaker (1976), Carnoy (1972), Purkey, Graves,
Zellner (1970), and others, that these factors—reflected in the quality of life
found in and around schools—have a significant relationship to student
self-esteem and student achievement.

Traditionally, the quality of educational plants, programs, and policies have been treated as variables important primarily for their relationship to student achievement. Recently, however, a number of researchers (Epstein and McPartland, 1976; Gerber, 1982) have looked at student
satisfaction as a separate, important outcome of schooling in its own right.
As Rosenshine and McGaw (1972) maintain, "Teacher behaviors which demean,
humiliate, or deny the rights of students may be judged wrong despite any
evidence that these behaviors promote desired outcomes. The end does not justify
the means" (p. 641). We would expand this statement to include not only behaviors but also places, policies, and programs. Inviting schools are places where
people enjoy teaching and learning, and where policies and programs contribute
to this joy. Student and teacher satisfaction not only lead to academic achievement
but are also legitimate goals in and of themselves.

This final chapter presents a model of what we consider to be an
inviting school. To do this, we contrast two models suggested by our
colleague Hal G. Lewis: the *efficient factory* and the *inviting family*. We
believe that preference for one over the other greatly influences the total
quality of life in schools. Both models have merit for schools and are not so
much discrete entities as two aspects of a continuum. However, we believe
that people, places, policies, and programs in education have strayed too
far from the inviting family model and too close to the efficient factory one.
Perhaps by presenting an inviting family model the present dominance of
the other will be lessened. The analogy can be pushed too far, of course, but
let us investigate it.

The Efficient Factory

There are many differences among factories, but most factories place emphasis on the following six characteristics: (1) mass production, (2) uniform product, (3) cost effectiveness, (4) technology, (5) centralized control, and (6) workers as functionaries. Let us consider these characteristics in turn.

Mass Production

In the efficient factory a large number of units, all alike, are turned out by assembly lines. In some cases, depending on the needs of society or the promotional activities of the sales department, minor differences in appearance and performance are introduced. But these differences are in various models and not in individual units coming off the line. The major emphasis is on quantity. Raw materials are graded, hammered, shaped, processed, conditioned, and turned into a standard and uniform product.

Uniform Product

The efficient factory is supervised closely to ensure that each product meets minimum standards of sameness. The process involves experts who are charged with ensuring quality control. These many experts monitor, sample, test, and approve or reject goods. Products that are damaged in the factory process, or that differ in any significant way, are rejected and shoved aside. These rejects will later be recycled, destroyed, or marked down and sold at discount as irregulars, odd lots, close-outs, or seconds, often without brand name or identification. These inferior goods, sometimes found in factory outlets, damaged goods stores, or discount houses, failed to meet the minimum required standards of uniformity.

Cost Effectiveness

In the efficient factory a high priority is given to cost effectiveness. The aesthetics of the plant is relatively unimportant. Factories are designed without windows to control the climate, reduce maintenance, and prevent vandalism and theft. Efficient factories are often surrounded by chain-link fences topped with barbed wire, with gates and guards on duty around the clock, again to prevent theft and vandalism. Cost corners are cut wherever possible, and short-term profits are sometimes given priority over long range planning. In almost every policy decision, costs are the bottom line.

Technology

Technological advances are greatly valued in the efficient factory and are introduced into plants as quickly as possible. Considerable attention is paid to such hardware items as computers, automatic equipment, programmed delivery systems, and other inventions designed to provide swift and sure processing procedures. Even workers are seen as physical objects to be combined with the latest machinery to provide still more technological efficiency.

Centralized Control

In the efficient factory, planning is usually separated from production. Authority flows from the top down, from board to executives, to production managers, to plant superintendents, to supervisors, and finally to workers. Policies and programs are traditionally developed in places and by people far removed from the production line in function and status, if not in distance. Managers and workers have their respective functions and pre-rogatives, and workers have little voice in planning. Workers get what they can by organizing, bargaining, and when necessary by striking. But whatever workers get, it usually does not include a role in policy formulation of program design. This formulation is done by boards of directors, executive management, and design experts.

Workers as Functionaries

Workers in the efficient factory are expected to be punctual, obedient, conforming, and above all *busy*. Individual needs, interests, and personalities are relatively unimportant. Work is broken into small, easy-to-understand, mistake-proof tasks. The workers are controlled by clocks, bells, buzzers, whistles, shifts, public address systems, assembly lines, and a host of supervisors. Efficiency studies are made regularly to monitor the entire process to ensure maximum production. Meanwhile, public relations departments project the image of the happy worker.

These characteristics of efficient factories are certainly not comprehensive or universal, but they do suggest the organizational nature of the industrial plant. Such organization has produced an avalanche of material goods, much of it good and some of it shoddy. In return for the cornucopia of products, North America has paid a heavy price in the way of human suffering and discontent and of environmental pollution and destruction.

We now turn our attention to the way the efficient factory model has been adopted in school—which is a little eerie.

The Efficient Factory School

Let us take each of the six factory characteristics described and look at its counterpart in schools.

Mass Production

The sheer size of schools has been increased so that some now enroll students by the thousands. As in the efficient factory, quantity takes precedence over quality, and minimal standards take priority over optimal goals. Curricula are established and requirements are made to ensure that all students take certain subjects and get certain basic material in a mass lock-step procedure based on outcome variables.

Uniform Product

Perhaps never before in North American education has there been such emphasis placed on uniform product. Testing experts are everywhere, and *performance indicators, exit skills, behavioral objectives,* and *minimal competencies* have entered the language. Uniform productivity is insured by "mandated" pupil achievement, minimal competency tests, exit skills at each "learning station," and frequent performance testing on "objective" multiple choice tests. Nonconforming students are recycled by being made to repeat grades. If they do manage to make it through high school, students who do not meet minimum academic standards may be given a certificate of attendance rather than a high-school diploma. Other nonconforming students may be ejected totally from the learning environment, as in the case of suspensions, expulsions, and the like.

Cost Effectiveness

Like efficient factories, many schools place highest priority on cost effectiveness. Aesthetic considerations are relatively unimportant. Schools are designed without windows to save heat, reduce maintenance, and prevent vandalism. Frills are kept to a minimum or eliminated completely, along with special programs that do not pay their own way. Educational policies are made in terms of cost effectiveness, and only those programs that are cost effective survive.

Technology

North American education is a major market for hardware designed to instruct students more efficiently and effectively. This is particularly true in the efficient factory school. Early on, students are introduced to "instructional centers" and "learning labs" boasting technological advances such as closed circuit television, talking typewriters, tape decks, listening stations, audiovisual packages, and microcomputers. Teachers and students are surrounded by kits, units, modules, sets, packs, printers, and other expensive devices. Teachers are encouraged to instruct through the use of pack-

aged, highly structured programs. At every turn, technological developments influence the educational process.

Centralized Control

Superintendents, school boards, state departments of education, and
even the federal government are mandating standards for students,
teachers, and other persons who work in schools. This standardizing process is supported in the efficient factory school as a necessary part of the
organizational structure. Professional relationships are hierarchical, with a
flow of authority from the top down, from school board to superintendent,
to principal or supervisor, to teacher, and then to students. As is typically
the case with remote administrative authority, there is usually a wide gulf
between the *mandators* and the *mandated.* The result can be that teachers
and students begin to burn out and become uncaring automatons.

Workers as Functionaries

In the efficient factory school, teachers and students have relatively
little control over their workaday lives. Entries and exits are controlled by
schedules and punctuated by bells. What is to be taught and learned, as well
as why, how, when, and to or by whom, is determined by textbook writers,
accrediting agencies, state department officials, directors of curriculum,
university consultants, or active pressure groups. Usually, learning is defined in terms of basic skill mastery, performance on standardized tests, or
behavioral objectives designed by people far removed from the classroom.
Students and teachers are expected to be docile, hard-working, and respon-
sive to the needs of the system..

Keeping the foregoing six characteristics of the efficient factory
model in mind, let us now turn to a second model, that of the inviting
family.

The Inviting Family

As we mentioned in Chapter 1, the word *invitation* comes from the
Latin *invitare,* which means "to summon cordially, not to shun." This
meaning may be vital to positive family relationships where each family
member is cordially summoned to realize his or her unique potential and
where no one in the family is shunned. In our view, the inviting family has at
least five basic characteristics: (1) respect for individual uniqueness, (2)
cooperative spirit, (3) sense of belonging, (4) pleasing habitat, and (5)
positive expectations. Let us examine these five qualities more closely.

Respect for Individual Uniqueness

In the inviting family there is an appreciation of individual differences. Not everyone is expected to be alike or to do the same thing. There is tolerance for family members who are unable or unwilling to meet family expectations or aspirations. "He's not heavy, he's my brother" reflects this attitude of support. There is also a great and shared pride in those who exceed the fondest hopes of the family. Flexible and varied work periods are promoted as each family member moves toward his or her own creative ways of being. In the inviting family, the concept of *each is unique* determines family policy.

Cooperative Spirit

"One for all and all for one" describes the inviting family. Adults and children learn from each other. The family is seen by all its members as a cooperative enterprise in which cooperation is valued far more than competition. When one member achieves, all members feel a part of the success. And when one member is having difficulty, it is a family concern. Everyone pitches in to help until the person is able to catch up. In the inviting family, a special watch is kept for those in the family who might need a special boost. This support is always provided within a circle of unconditional respect for the feelings of those who may need assistance.

Sense of Belonging

A most important quality of the inviting family is a deep sense of belonging. This feeling is cultivated wherever possible. Family members spend time talking with each other and sharing their feelings and concerns. They make a special effort to look beyond their own immediate gratification to the needs of other family members. Everyone thinks in terms of *our* family, *our* home, *our* traditions, *our* responsibilities. This loyalty toward one another and the warmth felt for one another result in mutual appreciation, positive self-esteem, and a deep sense of family togetherness.

Pleasing Habitat

Aesthetics is given a high priority in the inviting family. Living green plants, attractive colors, comfortable furniture, soft lighting, open space, cleanliness, pleasant smells, fresh air, and comfortable temperatures are provided wherever possible. Changes in the physical environment are made regularly to keep the habitat attractive. The emphasis on creating an aesthetic environment, even in the most difficult situations, is beautifully illustrated by Betty Smith in her book *A Tree Grows in Brooklyn* (1943), in which a poor family obtains a piano at great effort and personal sacrifice. In the inviting family habitat, everything is designed to send the message "be as comfortable as possible, we're glad you're here."

Positive Expectations

Encouraging each family member to realize his or her unique potential is an important quality of the inviting family. Family members expect good things of themselves and others, but these expectations are always presented within an atmosphere of respect. Every effort is made to encourage feelings of self-control and individual responsibility and to encourage members to realize their physical, social, and psychological potential.

Now let us relate the inviting family to the inviting family school.

The Inviting Family School

The following five characteristics describe what we have chosen to call the *inviting family school*. They parallel the five basic qualities of the inviting family just presented.

Respect for Individual Uniqueness

A hallmark of the inviting family school is that judgments and evaluations are made primarily on a personal basis. Each child is seen as unique and is treated as such. Where grades are unavoidable, every effort is made to insure that the marking system is used for the welfare of the people involved. Students are encouraged to test themselves and judge their own personal performance and progress. Errors are viewed as a source of information rather than as a sign of failure. Further, students participate in making decisions about how grading and evaluation processes will be applied. All students are encouraged to take confidence in their ability to learn, to trust their feelings, and to celebrate their personal uniqueness.

Cooperative Spirit

In the inviting family school, peer teaching is encouraged so that both tutors and tutored may benefit. In every way, people in the school are expected to take cooperative responsibility for what happens in their lives. Everyone is expected to participate in the decision-making process. Teachers and students are not isolated from decision-making, but rather, in a very real sense, are "executives" of the school. A related feature of the inviting family school is that competition is minimized in favor of mutual support. Students who are unable to achieve as expected are offered extra help, always within an empathetic, respectful stance. School activities are based on cooperation and mutual concern.

Sense of Belonging

The inviting family school cherishes community warmth and togetherness. Students and teachers think in terms of *our* school, *our* work, and all of *us* together. Students are kept together with peers as much as possible. If one student must be removed from the group, it is for as short a period as possible. Every effort is made to encourage feelings of school pride and of being a member of a learning and caring community. Perhaps this sense of belonging can best be illustrated by one student's high-school experience: "Our school is like a big, caring family. When my father died all my teachers were at the funeral home. My senior class collected money and sent a wreath. I'll never forget their kindness."

Pleasing Habitat

A pleasant environment for living and learning is stressed in the inviting family school. The landscape, upkeep, and general appearance of the school are given careful attention. Teachers, staff, and students take *equal* responsibility with custodians to create and maintain an aesthetically pleasing physical environment. Regardless of the age of the school, everyone takes pride in maintaining it as attractively as possible. Extra efforts are made to ensure that lighting, acoustic qualities, temperature, room design, window areas, furniture arrangement, colors, use of space, displays, all make a contribution to an appealing and comfortable setting.

Positive Expectations

Efforts are made in the inviting family school to encourage favorable self-esteem. Students are taught that each person has relatively untapped capacities for learning, and that this learning is something that happens *inside* themselves; it is not something that happens *outside*. Students participate in deciding what they will study, how much they will learn, how fast they will learn, and how they will evaluate their own individual progress. Each student is encouraged by positive expectations communicated by teachers. These teachers, in turn, have a sense of personal efficacy and high expectations for themselves. Again, these expectations are manifested in terms of respect for oneself and others.

There is no specific blueprint for the creation of inviting family schools because each school, like each family, has its own unique characteristics. There is, however, as our colleague Dean Fink has pointed out, a general plan of action for developing inviting schools. This involves an awareness and understanding of invitational education, an application of the theory to specific situations, and a working together with all school personnel and students to develop inviting places, policies, and programs. Creating and maintaining inviting schools, as we have stressed, is a *being with* and *doing with* process and involves the perceptions, stance, and behaviors that have been presented throughout this book.

We believe that now more than ever there is a need for the development of inviting family schools. Efforts to create such schools are now underway throughout the United States and Canada. School systems as diverse as Horseheads, New York; Greensboro, North Carolina; Prince George's County, Maryland; Sarasota County, Florida; Council Bluffs, Iowa; Centerville, Ohio; and Halton County, Ontario, among others, have already started school programs to implement invitational theory. Further, hundreds of workshops and conferences have been conducted to introduce secretaries, superintendents, teachers, librarians, principals, supervisors, parents, nurses, and food-service professionals to invitational education.

Developing inviting schools is no easy task, and the results are not guaranteed. We do believe that the effort is worthwhile, and that the cost of educational success with anything less is much too expensive. We hope you will join with us and others to help make our schools "the most inviting places in town."

Conclusion

In this book we have explored the process of inviting school success. By focusing on the subtle but pervasive messages extended to students in the school environment, this book has emphasized something familiar that has heretofore been overlooked. "You cannot miss the road to the City of Emerald," said the witch in *The Wizard of Oz,* "for it is paved with yellow brick." But Emerald Cities, like invitations in schools, can sometimes be too obvious to see.

Four unhappy characters went to find the Wizard of Oz: a scarecrow who thought he had no brain, a tin woodsman who thought he had no heart, a lion who believed he had no courage, and a young girl who thought she lacked the power to make changes in her life. All were under the delusion that if they could only reach the Great and Terrible Oz, he would grant them the things they lacked. Little did they realize that they already possessed the very things they sought. When the four finally accomplished what they believed they could never do—kill the Wicked Witch of the West—they returned to the Emerald City impatient for their rewards. There they discovered that wizards (like teachers) have no magic power.

Yet, the wizard did manage to do things "that everybody knows can't be done." He cared about people, and to each of the four he sent a most powerful invitation: "A testimonial! A decree!" He invited them to see things in themselves that they had overlooked and to use what they already possessed. As Dorothy said when she finally got back to Kansas: "Oh, Aunt Em, I've been to many strange and marvelous places looking for something that was right here all along . . . right in my own backyard!"

So it is with inviting school success.

Appendix A

INVITING SCHOOL SUCCESS

There are as many practical ways to invite school success as there are people in and around schools who have imagination and who *want* to invite themselves and others to realize their potential. The following lists contain over two hundred suggestions, which are only examples of these ways. Please consider and choose those that may fit your style and your situation. Any group of professionals electing to do so can come together and create a list of suggestions as good or better than these.

The focus of *Inviting School Success* is on the classroom teacher, but everything in schools is connected to everything else. The way the school bus driver treats a student affects how well that student does in class. The manner in which the food is prepared and served in the cafeteria influences what role the principal will play that day. Because of these countless interrelationships, the following lists have been divided into categories illustrating what the elementary teacher, the food service professional, the physical educator, the middle-school teacher, the school administrator, the school bus driver, the school counselor, the secretary, and the secondary-school teacher can do to make schools more inviting places for people.

These lists are dedicated to the single, isolated teacher who is determined to make school more inviting. They offer a good beginning to answering the question this teacher may be asked by fellow professionals: "What can I do to help make our school the most inviting place in town?"

What Elementary-School Teachers Can Do

1. *Build momentum*   Before school begins, when you first receive your class roster, send a postcard to each of your incoming students. A brief note letting each child know that you are looking forward to the pleasure of his or her company is a fine way to start the school year.

2. *Hold a "young-parent tea party"*   Parents who are sending a child to school for the first time often have fears and anxieties about "losing" their children. It can be most helpful if these parents are invited to tea and shown what their children will experience. This is also an excellent way to recruit volunteers for parent aides.

3. *Give an apple on opening day*   We've all heard of an apple for the teacher. Well, switch things around, and on opening day of school have an apple on the desk of each student in your class. This can be a specific way of saying: "How glad I am to have you here, and how much we will learn together this year."

4. *Get off to a fast start*   Children come to school the first day very excited, expecting to learn to read and write. Don't disappoint them. Duplicate a very simple, brief paragraph story with several blanks. "I go to _____school. My teacher's name is _____." Write the answers on the

board and practice. Students can take their papers home and exclaim: "Look what I learned to read and write today." You are off to a great start.

5. *Take turns reading* When students take turns reading aloud, the teacher can speed things up, and add to the excitment, by reading aloud after each student. This keeps the pace fast and avoids boredom.

6. *Make individual chalkboards* Cut pressed wood, masonite board, or similar material and paint with blackboard paint. Each child works on his or her own board, then holds the board up for the teacher to check silently. This results in a private communication between student and teacher, for no one can read another board without turning.

7. *Build a loft* Children love snug places, and few places are as comfortable as a loft built across one end of the classroom. (Groups of parents can help with construction.) A loft gives more classroom space, makes a fine corner for small group meetings, a time-out area, or even plays. Sometimes, carpet companies will donate remnants for covering the floor and steps.

8. *Be positive* Too often directions are negative: "Don't talk," "Stay seated," "Stop running," "Quit that." Try making directions positive by focusing on what *should* be done, rather than on what should *not* be done.

9. *Raid the clothes closet* To help break the ice with a group of students, ask each to bring to class (or wear if appropriate) a favorite article of clothing. Ask each participant to explain how this particular article became a favorite. You will find there is a story in every closet.

10. *Rotate the seating* When working with smaller children, it helps to rotate the seating from time to time so that each child has the opportunity to sit close to the teacher. This also helps to equalize psychological distance.

11. *Arrange a "down-time" corner* An overstuffed armchair, a rocking chair, or even an old bathtub piled with pillows, along with a rug, books, and a game or two, can be just the thing to help a student overcome anxieties or anger stemming from some temporary crisis in his or her life.

12. *Lay a class carpet* Ask each student to bring in one or two pieces of carpet squares. The class can arrange the squares according to their own creativity. The squares can then be fastened to the floor. The carpet will cut down noise, make the room cozier in winter, and provide a fine place to settle down for storytelling or reading.

13. *Maintain a costume closet* Old hats, uniforms, costumes, masks, and unusual clothing can be used for class plays, role-playing activities, self-directed dramatizations, and related activities. Such activities are particularly successful in the teaching of reading. (Yard sales are a great source of supply.)

14. *Maintain a mail service* A mailbox somewhere in the class-room enables students to send notes to each other and to the teacher. Also, the teacher can use the mailbox to communicate positive messages to students. (To ensure that some student is not overlooked, the teacher can keep a private roster of student names to check off as notes are sent.)

15. *Assign "can-do" homework* Homework should be assigned in which the student has a good chance of success. To assign homework when there is reason to believe that students cannot do it is simply causing trouble. The secret is to assign homework that you *know* students can do. When they ask why, you reply: "Practice, practice, practice is the key to learning."

16. *Build interest in spelling* A good way to combine social rela-tionships with basic spelling skills is to use the first name of each child in spelling lists. This encourages students to get to know each other while learning how to spell.

17. *Dial-a-parent* Each week call a parent with some honest and positive report about his or her child. If the parent does not have a telephone, a post-card with the same report will work as well.

18. *Teach something tough* One of the best ways to invite students to feel good about themselves as learners is to teach them something that others do not know. This is particularly important when working with students labeled *slow* and placed in special classes. In teaching spelling, for example, the teacher may include a few very difficult words, such as *proselytize* or *proletariat,* that even the so-called bright students will not know. Few things are as enhancing as knowledge, particularly when stu-dents are trying desperately to avoid the label *slow learner* or *retard.*

19. *Use the newspaper* Watch the newspaper for articles dealing with students and families, their interests, and the course content. Clipping newspaper articles and sharing them with students—even sending a holi-day or other special greeting to the class by placing a classified ad in the local paper—can be effective both as a means of expressing positive feel-ings and as a way of encouraging students to read.

20. *Share collections* Almost every student has collected some-thing—cans, rocks, dolls, matchbox covers. Collecting can lead to all sorts of marvelous learning and future careers. Encourage students to begin collections. If a student already has a collection, invite him or her to display it in the school.

21. *Make an I Can* Cover a small fruit-juice can with bright contact paper. Paste a picture of an eye cut from a magazine on the outside of the can. When a student says "I can't," give the student an *I Can.* The I Can is good to keep pencils in and to remind the student that "I can!"

22. *Avoid the /wh/ bird*   When working with young children it is helpful to avoid an overabundance of *who, what,* or *why* questions. The young child is likely to interpret such questions as an accusation that he or she has done something wrong.

23. *Eat the alphabet*   Kindergarten and first-grade children can have the fun of finding a food that begins with a certain letter. Start with *A* (apple? angel-food cake?) and try to work through the alphabet, one letter at a time. Of course, the students help in finding the right letters!

24. *Spread positive rumors*   Take note of something positive a student does, then describe it to the class without mentioning the student's name. The purpose of positive rumors is to let students know how good they are and how much they can learn. When a teacher remarks: "I noticed how courteous a certain student was this morning," the entire class is complimented.

25. *Wish happy summer birthdays*   Sometimes people in schools who have summer birthdays get neglected. To avoid this, on the last day of school have all summer birthday people stand while everyone sings "Happy Birthday" to them.

What Food-Service Professionals Can Do

1.   *Use bright, warm colors to invite*   This is true in even the most meager surroundings. Bright color is a real pick-up for the school cafeteria. Invite the students and faculty for a paint party on a Saturday morning. You supply the brunch.

2.   *Offer comfortable seating*   Your seating arrangement can have a definite effect on atmosphere. Make sure there is adequate space between tables. It is recommended to have eighteen inches between chair backs when diners are seated.

3.   *Have music*   Soft, appropriate music can make the time spent in your cafeteria more relaxing. It could even brighten your steps!

4.   *Hang live plants*   Attractive hanging baskets and other plants make any cafeteria come alive. They can help develop a homey atmosphere in your cafeteria. Students can help with their care.

5.   *Remember your basics of menu planning*   Consider the food characteristics of color, texture, consistency, flavor combination, shape, and method of preparation. Do the combinations from your menu make an attractive and pleasing wholesome meal?

6.   *Consider the appearance of your food*   Appearance alone can be changed by the garnishes and condiments used with food. Try something different, such as fresh fruit and vegetables. Be imaginative!

7.   *Remember that variety is the spice of life*   Offering the same foods over and over is one of the most common faults in menu planning. Experiment, use foods that are in season, and take a chance! You and your guests may be pleasantly surprised.

8.   *Provide caloric information*   What are the calories of the entrees and other items being served? This information will be particularly useful to weight-conscious persons.

9.   *Offer specific combinations of low-calorie plates*   You could even provide a few nutrition-education tidbits to go along with them.

10.   *Celebrate birthdays*   Prepare a big sheet cake once a month for students whose birthdays fall on that month. If you have the energy, you could have a cupcake for each birthday student.

11.   *Work with the community*   Get involved with special community activities. Make a special day to honor older adults by having students invite their grandparents or an older adult to visit the school and have lunch.

12.   *Seek out assistance*   Discover new information from your colleagues. Visit other school cafeterias. Join professional organizations. Keep abreast with the latest technology and ideas in both nutrition and food service.

13.   *Have taste tests*   Students can help judge on a regular basis. This will allow students and food service staff to get better acquainted, will encourage the students to see how the kitchen operates, and most importantly, will function as a source of student input.

14.   *Work through student groups*   These are usually the leaders of the school and can certainly help to make the cafeteria more inviting. You might even organize a student food-service professional club.

15.   *Smile!*   A friendly smile from each food-service professional can add to the flavor of any meal.

16.   *Keep fresh bulletin boards*   Attractive bulletin boards in the cafeteria that are bright, up-to-date, and informative can add to learning and to the beauty of the area.

17.   *Remember the holidays*   Holidays are sprinkled throughout the school year. They offer special ways to invite creatively. Halloween, Thanksgiving, Christmas, and Passover are only a few of the many special events that can be celebrated with special foods, decorations, and themes.

18.   *Make the kitchen a learning center*   Many classes can benefit from visiting the kitchen and learning about food preparation procedures. This is also a good way to teach sanitation. In high school a visit can be used

to provide special training for students interested in food service. They can function as cashiers, typists, cooks, clerks, and servers.

19. *Give some choices* It seems wasteful to give each person the *same* amount of the *same* food. Find ways to allow students to have choices. With planning, it can be done!

20. *Toot your horn* The cafeteria menus can be placed in newspapers, announcements, bulletin boards, or even announced with the morning PA news.

21. *Remember National School Lunch Week* This is a good time to host parents. A special program can promote the school lunch program and give parents an opportunity to have lunch with their children.

22. *Fly the school colors* Where reasonable, use the school colors in bulletin boards, painted walls, even, on special occasions, the food!

23. *Greet your guests* Have at least one person to speak a friendly greeting to each student as he or she moves down the cafeteria line. And do not forget a thank-you at the cash end.

24. *Celebrate other cultures* Chinese, Mexican, Hawaiian, West Indian, Italian, and German cultures are only some of the many whose foods you can salute with your menu. With a little planning, your menu can reflect the academic curriculum.

25. *Wear special uniforms* We are all familiar with the standard white outfit worn by most food-service professionals. But why not pastels once in awhile? Also, whatever the uniform of the day might be, it can be accented for special times such as Christmas, Halloween, and Thanksgiving. Also, an attractive apron can do wonders for the most sterile-looking white uniform.

What Middle-School Teachers Can Do

1. *Prime the pump* Initial contacts with students are very important. Call, if possible, or write each student even before school starts. Introduce yourself and welcome the student to *our* school. Invitations can start early.

2. *Share decisions* Where possible, involve others in the decision-making process. Students can participate in such areas as rules of conduct, academic expectations, activities, even textbook reviews and teacher selection. The main point is to make it *our* school, where *we* have some influence on what happens to *us*.

3. *Solve the mystery* A good ice-breaker is to invite the class members to write something about themselves that is *unusual*. These clues

should be written in sentence form and the folded clues placed in a box. Pass the clues to each person, each receiving one clue. Now, all "detectives" try to locate their person.

4. *Start a trading library*   Set up a small library in your classroom where students can donate books and take turns serving as librarian. Explain to students that books are meant to be used and enjoyed. The library promotes both sharing and reading.

5. *Form some triads*   Divide your class into groups of threes called *triads*. Ask each triad to research, obtain materials, and teach a minilesson on the selected course subject. Triads invite new friendships, break down barriers, and encourage learning.

6. *Communicate positively*   Too often the majority of messages sent to parents are essentially negative: "Bill forgot his gym socks," "Lucy was late again." To avoid emphasizing the negative, make a vow that most personal notes going home will be positive: "Bill is making great progress in rope-climbing," "Lucy has written some beautiful little poems." In a child's life there are no little successes or failures—everything counts.

7. *Keep on schedule*   A small clock somewhere in your classroom will help to budget your time and energies. In an office, it is best to place the clock behind the chair the guest will use so you can be aware of time schedules without consulting your wristwatch—which can be a very disinviting act.

8. *Lower the volume*   If you are one who raises your voice when the discipline begins to break down, then practice *lowering* your voice when you want attention. The surprise works almost every time.

9. *Demonstrate your fallibility*   Be willing to express your own lack of knowledge on a particular subject, and to ask students for help in arriving at understandings. By modeling that "no one is perfect," you invite students to risk trying and making mistakes in order to develop.

10. *Cool down first*   Teachers who practice invitational education avoid responding to a situation while angry or upset. It is important to let tempers cool down a little before answering, particularly when you're putting something in writing.

11. *Relate to people, not labels*   Be cautious in substituting the label for the person. For example, a person might be exhibiting very disinviting behavior, but this does not mean that the person is a disinviting person. Sometimes labels can be worse than the problem itself.

12. *Post college offerings*   Keep up to date on classes taught at neighboring colleges and universities, particularly in your professional field. By posting these offerings, you invite your fellow professionals to take advantage of them as well. Better still, organize a carpool for attending them.

13. *Hold a fractions party*   Bring (or ask the class to bring) some pies, square cakes, or other goodies and invite students to recognize the differences among ¾, ⅝, ½, or ⅓. (They get to eat their answers.) It will not take long for every student to learn there is quite a difference between ⅔ and ⅓!

14. *Sock it to 'em*   Ask each student to bring an old sock to school. Place the sock over a shoe and wear it for a walk. Next, wet all the socks and place them in the sun. Something will soon grow! This little exercise invites student interest in the natural sciences.

15. *Build a poem*   Writing a sixteen-line poem can seem like an impossible task to some students. To avoid the problem, ask each student to write a *one*-line poem on an agreed-upon topic (a sunset is an excellent subject). Collect the one-line poems and select a small group of students to put the lines into a poem. The result is usually outstanding.

16. *Place a mirror on the wall*   Obtain a full-length mirror and place it somewhere in the classroom where students can see themselves as they pass by. This promotes neatness and a sense of grooming among young people.

17. *Visit a graveyard*   To encourage writing and imagination, take a field trip to an old graveyard. Ask the students to study the stones, then select one to write about. "What was the person like? What happened in his or her life? How was life at that time?" Higher-grade students can even conduct actual research in library files, old newspapers, and the like.

18. *Take a sound walk*   Invite your studnts to take a *sound walk* with you. Have each student take a piece of paper and sit in a quiet place. Ask the students to list all the sounds they can hear that occur in nature. Also, list on the same paper all the sounds made by humans. Later, they can pair off and compare their answers, and then pairs can join other pairs to share.

19. *Invite writing*   Ask students to write stories about themselves. Collect the stories along with poems and drawings and bind them with laminated cardboard. The completed books can be taken home as gifts, or placed in the school library for others to check out. The process encourages writing and a special feeling of importance.

20. *Buy greetings at half price*   Christmas, Hanukkah, Valentine's Day, and other holiday cards always go on sale immediately after the holiday is over. This is a very good time to buy cards for next year's mailing to students, colleagues, and friends.

21. *Discover a salad bar*   Check around and locate a restaurant that provides a luncheon salad bar. If you and your colleagues are able to leave campus during lunch, form a luncheon party. An inexpensive and refreshing salad luncheon is good for you and provides a pleasant time for mutual support and professional development.

22. *Begin a museum*   Start a special file of letters, awards, or treasures that you have received during your teaching career. When you begin to feel a little blue or begin to doubt your own worth, visit your museum. It will lift your spirits, renew your faith in your own ability, and help you to help others.

23. *Handle the unacceptable*   When a student has submitted something unacceptable, try this approach: "I think you can do better than this." Point out ways the work can be improved, then say: "Will you try again?" This encourages both student responsibility and academic success.

24. *Swap a teacher*   Arrange to trade positions with a teacher from another school for a week. This will enrich everyone—the school, the teacher who volunteers to participate, and the students involved. It is a good way to avoid the early spring "blahs."

25. *Maintain a model classroom*   Classrooms are usually stripped of all decorations during the summer to allow workers to clean and paint. Summer is often the time when new students and parents visit the school, so suggest that the classroom closest to the office be beautifully decorated during summer. The principal can take incoming students and parents to this room to show them how inviting the whole school will look come fall.

What Physical Educators Can Do

1. *Share a lap*   When most of us were growing up, being ordered by the coach to "take a lap" in gym class was a form of punishment. It can be made into a treat when the student is invited by the coach to "Take a lap with me." Jogging around the track with the coach can build a fine sense of fellowship.

2. *Play that funky music*   Use music to add tempo to warm-up exercises. Let students bring their favorite records in to provide the beat to which they move as they exercise. This adds a new and exciting dimension to exercising and can help make an otherwise boring activity somewhat exciting and fun.

3. *Share stuff*   In the classroom health part of physical education (grades 7 through 9), maintain a collection of health magazines, books, and articles as well as sports literature that may be of interest to the age group for check-out or free-time reading.

4. *Have a manager for each week*   Encourage group and individual responsibility and cooperation by inviting a group of students (or an individual student) to be your assistants for a week. Encourage your assistants to share in planning the week's activities as well as supervising equipment.

5. *Keep students up*   Keep students abreast of what is happening in the news in terms of sports and physical activities. Information about sports tournaments, such as the World Series, the Super Bowl, or national events, may promote interest and prompt reading. On special occasions, such as the Olympics, present a mini-unit on the history of the event and the training involved.

6. *Keep the gym fresh*   Solicit the janitor's and maid's special help in having pride in helping to keep the gym, locker rooms, and shower areas as clean and fresh-smelling as possible. Doing your part in cleaning may invite extra effort on the custodian's part. Also, the words *please* and *thank you* will encourage the special help you need in keeping the gym clean.

7. *Be audiovisual minded*   Use physical education activity films as a change of pace in teaching. Let students see the various steps in accomplishing a specific skill. If available, use a videotape machine. This tool provides excellent feedback and allows each student to see the benefits of working together as well as measuring individual progress.

8. *Bring the history of sports to life*   Ask students to draw posters depicting historical aspects or highlights of the particular sport in season. This is also applicable to special or unusual events in sports. This may be used effectively to introduce a new sports activity that is being taught or to point out little-known facets of a traditional sport.

9. *Show the world of sports*   To add excitement and invite learning, secure special film highlights (usually free of charge) of sporting events such as the World Series, the Super Bowl, or the Olympics. Your students are likely to be inspired to new heights of achievement by watching these exciting events.

10. *Lend a helping hand*   If physical education uniforms are required, try to provide (in a discreet manner) clean used or new uniforms for those who cannot afford them. In most schools this is easily approved by the administration.

11. *Invite new students*   When a new student enrolls in class, take a few minutes before class to find out a few pertinent and positive things, such as what town the student has come from, personal interests, whether the student is an athlete or club member, and where the student resides now. Then introduce the student to the class and share positive tidbits of information.

12. *Go on activity trips*   Arrange outside trips in conjunction with a teaching unit. For example, provide the opportunity for games at a bowling alley, roller rink, ice-skating arena, putt-putt golf, or even a tour of a regulation golf course. It is also relatively easy to arrange group attendance at nearby college varsity sports activities.

13. *Look for the causes of problems* It is important to work on causes of problems in schools. These causes are not always student misbehavior. For example, being late to class from a shower in physical education may be caused by late dismissal from gym, or there may not be enough time allowed for class changing. Changing the system or reevaluating your actions can sometimes eliminate problems.

14. *Try an alphabet soup exercise* One way to avoid boredom when directing calisthenics is to divide students into groups of three. Next, call out a letter in the alphabet and ask each triad to make that letter using their bodies.

15. *Improve the office* Provide an attractive, uncluttered office (as best you can) with signs inviting students to come in. In the best interests of teaching and privacy, it may help to indicate specific times (office hours) when you are more available for chatting and personal discussions.

16. *Keep the vision* See students as they can be, not as they are. Too often physical educators say: "Do your best" when "You can do better, so *practice*" can be a more powerful invitation to realize potential. Every student is in the process of becoming, so it is important for physical educators to invite them to become in positive directions.

17. *Vary your grading system* Grading systems can be modified to place major emphasis on effort, attitude, cooperation, and sportsmanship. You might discover that if you have the students work on these aspects of their development, the skill and performance aspects of physical education will fall into place.

18. *Be a social director* Periodically provide opportunities for teachers to participate right along with students. These may include such social activities as basketball free-throw shooting contests, Ping-Pong, or golf. These activities provide the means by which teacher-teacher and teacher-student social interactions are encouraged.

19. *Watch for help signs* Watch for I-need-help signs among the students. If you notice a student who wants to learn a skill but is having difficulty doing so, discreetly offer to help after class or after school.

20. *Invite variety* Vary the standard rules of traditional games in creative ways. This takes some of the rigidity out of the expected and increases participation, success, and excitement.

21. *Be a showcase for talent* Provide opportunities for a school-wide display of acquired skills or talents such as tumbling, gymnastics, or modern dance. Strive for group recognition and effort as well as individual spotlighting. These opportunities for displaying students' talents come at school assemblies, PTA programs, and community club meetings.

22. *Advertise the activities of your students* Use the school newspaper to communicate special activities, awards, and events taking place in your physical education class. These may include the names of assistants, student of the week or month, skills records, feats, and accomplishments. Notations may be made of special sporting events coming up within the school or community as well as listings of the schedule of upcoming physical education activities.

23. *Post class achievements and honors* Assign one of the bulletin boards in the gym the special title of Physical Education Bulletin Board. Note any skills records, accomplishments, and feats of students in your class. Names and pictures of physical education assistants and specially recognized students may be displayed here also. It may even be fun to take a class photograph early in the year and post it. Then you have it to look back on as the year progresses.

24. *Invite special interests* Help form and sponsor special interest groups such as a jogging club (in the morning before school, at lunchtime, or after school), a bike-riding club for those who cycle to school (after school and weekends), or a sports event club to decorate bulletin boards on the sports in season. This group might also be responsible for posting a calendar of coming school and local sports events such as foot races, bike races, gymnastics club tryouts, or a school Ping-Pong tournament and related activities.

25. *Place positive signs in the gym* Signs such as Welcome to Massey Hill Junior High School, and Please Place Used Towels in Hamper request cooperation and are much more pleasant than signs telling people what not to do.

What School Administrators Can Do

1. *Organize a back-to-school party* Plan a faculty and staff party to take place before school begins. This coming together can be a simple covered-dish, BYOB sort of get-together to renew friendships, introduce new colleagues, and set the stage for a successful academic year.

2. *Celebrate each day* When each new school day begins the school administrator can walk around the school, salute the buses as they arrive, check the grounds, and make a special point of stopping at every classroom to say "Good morning" to students and teachers. (If the administrator is really energetic, he or she can say "So long, see you tomorrow" to students as they depart for home each day.). This habit invites a good feeling in students and faculty.

3. *Jack up the faculty meeting* Everyone can make a vow that all faculty meetings will start on time and will never go over one hour. One

simple technique to enforce the rule is for everyone to stand at the fifty-five-minute mark and continue standing until the end of the meeting. It will not go over an hour!

4. *Improve the teacher's lounge*   Teachers benefit from having a comfortable place to relax. Do what you can to make the lounge more inviting. A living plant, a bowl of flowers, an area rug, fresh paint, clean windows, a baked cake are among the many things that can make the "recovery room" more like a real place to relax.

5. *Float the faculty meeting*   Move the faculty meeting around the school and meet in different environments. This gives a freshness to meetings and a new outlook on problems. It also helps to get everyone involved. And no matter where you meet, remember to arrange for something to eat and drink. The "care and feeding" of faculty is most important. Even such simple fare as coffee, juice, cookies, and fruit can contribute to a successful meeting.

6. *Share successes*   Begin each faculty meeting with a report of all the honest success experiences that have taken place since the last meeting. Ask teachers and other professionals to share their success experiences. This process helps to start each meeting off on a positive note.

7. *Visit the provinces*   The school administrator is responsible for the entire school, not just the principal's office. Visit the teacher's lounge, gym, cafeteria, furnace room, shops, labs, classrooms, and grounds frequently. Discipline is best handled *before* it becomes a problem and the secret is to be visible. Besides, you don't need an invitation to visit your school!

8. *Be a booster*   The school administrator's time is severely limited, but his or her presence at a play, band concert, athletic contest, or other student activity can be seen as a most inviting act. When students (and parents) perceive the school administrator as intersted in their activities, they will probably feel more invited by the school.

9. *Invite action, not inaction*   Too often principals, like teachers, give directions that could best be followed by pet rocks: "*Don't* leave your class unattended," "*Stop* smoking in the faculty dining area," "*Quit* questioning school policies." Under such directions a pet rock would make the ideal teacher. Asking faculty and staff to do something is much better than telling them what not to do.

10. *Take a dare*   When the school plans a program involving faculty—faculty-student basketball game, skit program, fun night, raffle day—why not accept a part? Even though you can't do everything, you can always do something to make the family spirit come alive in your school.

11. *Send unconditional invitations*   Often we are guilty of sending invitations to students that suggest we really doubt acceptance. For ex-

ample, "You can join the club *if* you want to," "You are welcome, *but* we are leaving early," "I think you can learn this; *however,* you'll have to pay the price" all suggest conditional regard. It is usually better to send *unconditional* invitations, simple declarative statements of support: "I know you can do this."

12. *Be explicit with your invitations*   The more explicit a request, the more it lends itself to acceptance. Sometimes principals create misunderstandings by being vague, and others wonder "What was meant by that?" When the principal is explicit with his or her invitations, the likelihood of success increases. For example, the principal who says, "John, I want you to do this, will you do it?" has a good chance of having his or her invitation accepted.

13. *Invite cooperation with other schools*   If you wish to bring in a well-known speaker or consultant, one way to reduce the expense and responsibility involved is to ask neighboring school systems or related organizations to share in sponsoring the visit. This makes good money sense, encourages cooperation, increases attendance, and may result in your being invited by your educational neighbors at some later date.

14. *Use the yearbook*   School yearbooks are a great source of names and faces. By spending some time looking through the yearbook and relating names to faces, you'll be in a better position to learn the names of many of your students in a relatively short time and to practice using those names at every opportunity.

15. *Celebrate life*   Birthdays of students, teachers, and staff can be marked on a private calendar in readiness for a special greeting. (Even the grouchiest teacher will light up when he or she is given a surprise party.) And don't forget to celebrate the appearance of a new baby or other special event in the lives of students, staff, or faculty.

16. *Feed the feeders*   Send copies of honor rolls, student work, awards, outstanding papers, and related material to teachers in the feeder schools. This lets them know that you are aware of their major contributions to the success of your school.

17. *Keep a mug file*   Start a card file on members of the school's professional family, including teachers, aides, custodians, cafeteria staff, bus drivers, counselors—every adult who serves the school system. A single index card can hold a wealth of information about the people with whom the school administrator comes in contact. On each card list personal items, such as name of spouse, number of children, hobbies, interests. From time to time go through the file, add information, check that you have visited with everyone recently. If you have missed anyone, make a special effort to go and chat with that person. In a large school it is helpful to make a notation each time you visit with a person.

18. *Reduce line time*   Develop a plan that will permit faculty, staff, and students to avoid long lines in the cafeteria. Time in school is too valuable to spend in line. In fact, the time spent on learning tasks is one of the most important ingredients in children's success in school. A flexible lunch period schedule gives people a choice of what time they want to go to lunch. Parents can help with flexible lunch arrangements.

19. *Place some welcome decals*   The Midwest Specialties Company (P.O. Box 2026, Kalamazoo, Michigan 49001) sells decals for glass and solid doors. The decals read "Welcome to our school—Visitors please report to the main office upon entering the building during regular school hours. Thank you." This sign is certainly more professionally inviting than "Visitors Must Report to Office" or "No Trespassing."

20. *Recognize support personnel*   Crossing guards, bus drivers, cafeteria workers, custodians, and other noninstructional staff are vital to the school; let them know how important they are by inviting them to meetings, or have a luncheon or other special recognition for them. They all contribute significantly to the inviting or disinviting environment of the school.

21. *Organize a Saturday planting party*   Ask everyone in the school to come to school on a Saturday morning to help improve the appearance of the school with plants and flowers. Parents, students, and others can bring bedding plants. Even nurseries may donate a plant or two. School service clubs and garden clubs can also be invited to participate and join the party.

22. *Hold those calls*   When the school executive is with a visitor, it is a most inviting act for the executive to say to his or her secretary: "Will you please hold incoming calls for the next ten minutes?" This is an indirect way of saying to the visitor: "You are important, and for the next ten minutes, I do not want us to be interrupted.

23. *Say no slowly*   When you must give a negative response to a request, at least let it come after you have listened carefully and fully to the request. One of the worst indictments that can be leveled against an administrator is for someone to say: "The principal wouldn't even listen to me!" The failure even to consider a request, to hear the person out, can hurt more than the negative answer. Invite each person to express his or her request fully before it is accepted or rejected.

24. *Offer refreshments to visitors*   Breaking bread together is an ancient sign of peace and friendship. By offering each visitor to your office some coffee, tea, juice, or light refreshment, the stage is set for the resolution of problems and facilitation of good feelings.

25. *Improve teacher evaluations*   When the principal is planning to observe and evaluate a teacher, it is important to meet with the teacher first

and find out what the teacher plans to do. Looking at behavior only, and not at intentions as well, leaves out half the picture.

What School Bus Drivers Can Do

1. *Demonstrate leadership* Show the students on your bus by your *behavior* that you care about them, and explain why you need to set guidelines and limits on their activities. Avoid "Because I said so!" It is important that you express to your student riders the belief that they have as much value and responsibility as you do. Every person on the bus, including the driver, has equal value and deserves equal respect. Because it is *our* bus, we all have responsibility for making it a good place to be.

2. *Develop bus spirit* At the beginning of the school year invite your riders to decide upon a nickname for the bus. By using the same techniques as an athletic team, a group of riders and the driver can develop a real team spirit.

3. *Be a greeter* With each school day make it a point to say "Good morning" to each student as he or she steps on the bus. Each afternoon say "So long, see you tomorrow" as each student departs for home. This habit invites a good feeling in every one, *including* the driver.

4. *Start a chain reaction* The first student on the bus in the morning greets the next student who arrives; this continues until everyone is on the bus. This helps students to learn the names of their busmates and encourages a friendly environment on the bus.

5. *Use collective, inclusive words* Using such pronouns as *we, us,* and *our* on the bus is much more inviting than using *you, yours,* or *mine.* Make it *our* bus—keeping it clean is up to *us.* Using the collective term invites a feeling of shared effort.

6. *Point out what's working* Instead of always pointing out what is wrong, change your focus and point out things that are right. Bus riders learn much more from things that work than they do from things that do not.

7. *Be sensitive with praise* Not all students are willing or able to accept praise, particularly praise given to them in front of their friends. A private comment to let a student know how pleased you are with his or her behavior might be more appropriate.

8. *Show you care* When someone is ill or misses the bus for other reasons, a special comment to that student when he or she returns can be a most caring and thoughtful act.

9. *Keep up to date* Try to keep abreast of fads, fashions, heroes, films, sports, singers, and other current interest of students. This is a good way to show students the driver is with it.

10.   *Check the newspaper*   Watch the newspaper for articles dealing with your riders and their families. Clipping an article and sharing it with a student can be an effective way of expressing your interest.

11.   *Personalize some pencils*   For a few dollars it is possible to order pencils with some special greeting, such as "Season's Greetings to you from Mr. Smith." The pencils can be given to your riders the last day before a holiday season. The same idea can be used just before school ends for the summer: "Mrs. Reynolds wishes you a great summer vacation."

12.   *Double your pleasure*   As nice as it is to receive kind words directly, it can be even nicer to learn that kind words were spoken about you to someone else. Rather than praise someone directly, praising the person to someone else can have double the impact.

13.   *Divide the routes*   Although it is not always possible, buses could be made more inviting if they were smaller and had shorter routes. Having different sized buses and routes can benefit everyone and can give added flexibility to the school system.

14.   *Keep the bus clean*   Whether they admit it or not, most people enjoy riding in a clean bus. Do what you can to keep the bus clean, and encourage your riders to help. A little trash can or two on the bus (if not forbidden by regulations) can teach students good behavior.

15.   *Practice preventive maintenance*   Don't wait until the bus breaks down to take care of problems. Keep the bus in good running order by insisting on good service and safety checks.

16.   *Make repairs rather than patch-ups*   Torn seats with tape over them often lead to more torn seats. A professional patching kit works much better than tape. Catching damage early and repairing it well prevents the spread of further damage.

17.   *Check the system*   Sometimes the causes of problems in and around buses are not people. Sometimes is the *system*. Scheduling buses to leave school within a very few minutes after school ends each day forces students to run, shove, and push in order to make the bus.

18.   *Look sharp and tag up*   Driving a school bus is a professional responsibility and drivers should look the part. A metal name tag for each school bus driver together with a neat and well-groomed appearance identify drivers as professionals.

19.   *Keep rules short and simple*   Such simple rules as Please Remain in Seats, Please Respect Property, and Please Speak Softly can do wonders to maintain the driver's sanity. And remember, the fewer the rules, the less likely they are to be broken.

20. *Prepare a birthday box*   For the busy bus driver, a birthday box can be prepared during the summer months. The box contains small, inexpensive, wrapped gifts, nicely decorated. The birthday bus rider chooses a wrapped gift from the box for his or her own on that special day. On the last day of school, students with summer birthdays get to choose a wrapped gift.

21. *Make your bus inviting*   If not against rules, a little bulletin board, a smiley face, an animal cutout, design, or the like can invite the student to feel: "This is our bus. The driver takes pride in it, and so will I."

22. *Help arrange driving programs*   In addition to the usual driver education programs such as safety, maintenance, and the like, ask that training programs for bus drivers include such subjects as driver self-concept, interpersonal relationships, and stress management. This will work to everyone's benefit.

23. *Set an example in politeness*   *Please* and *thank you* are magic words. When the driver shows respect for the riders, it is likely that riders will begin to respect the driver. Civility and courtesy are critical in operating a bus.

24. *Stress cooperation*   Above everything else, driving a bus is a cooperative act. Without cooperation from other drivers, riders, and the public, driving a bus would be almost impossible. Encourage cooperation by *being* cooperative.

25. *Be safe*   The number one priority of a school bus driver is to safely transport children to and from school. More important than any of the above suggestions, the driver must be constantly alert to the safety of the riders. It is a special responsibility and honor to care for so many young lives. Practice safety in everything you do.

What School Counselors Can Do

1. *Brighten up the center*   Just because they stuck you in a closet is no reason it has to look like a closet! Hang posters, get some living green plants, make your office a place where people want to come. If you desire to be a professionally inviting counselor, have your counseling center reflect that desire. Have comfortable furniture for both students and adults and no thrones facing undersized chairs!

2. *Protect the single-parent child*   Sometimes schools can be discriminating against single-parent children. To guard against this, encourage faculty to ask their students, when engaged in gift-making during Mother's Day or Father's Day activities, to "make a card or gift for someone who is very important in your life." This gives a sense of belonging and purpose to the child who only has one parent, if that.

3. *Hold a professional sharing session*   Plan and conduct a "drop-by" session where teachers can enjoy refreshments and be involved in a brief training program on such topics as stress reduction, contract grading system, or other innovative offerings. It need not take long for some quality sharing.

4. *Honor older adults*   One way to honor senior citizens is to have a special day for grandparents and older adults. Students can send special invitations to their grandparents or older adult friends to visit the school, join in classes, and enjoy lunch. The day can be ended with a special assembly or class program.

5. *Arrange some luncheon dates*   Counselors can arrange to have lunch with a different person or group of persons each day. This can be alternated with administrators, teachers, and students. Breaking bread together and chatting informally can do a lot to improve interpersonal relations in the school.

6. *Check your timing*   Timing is very important in inviting. Too much, too soon, too little, too late can weaken the best invitation. Ask yourself: *What* invitation, by *whom,* is most likely to be accepted by *this* person at *this* time?

7. *Carpool an adventure*   Is a special lecture, important confer-ence, or other activity taking place in some other area? Perhaps the school can help pay for a meal and gas to send some personnel. When they return from the adventure they might share what they learned with the entire staff.

8. *Hold a faculty breakfast*   In return for a few dollars and a few hours of planning, the entire faculty can meet together for breakfast. If energies permit, perhaps the counselor and a few friends could fix break-fast for everyone. After all, service is what the helping profession is all about!

9. *Send a professional gift*   Need a special gift for a special friend? Subscribe to a professional magazine or journal to be sent to him or her. It is a gift that lasts all year.

10. *Float the bulletin board*   Obtain a large sheet of styrofoam. Place whatever message you select on it using mounted paper letters. Next, string several helium balloons to the bulletin board. You now have a floating bulletin board that can travel around the school, popping up at unexpected places.

11. *Give "expert" advice sparingly*   One of the basic tenets of invita-tional education is to recognize that every person has the potential of becoming more capable and self-supportive. For this reason, be reluctant

in providing ready answers to problems. Counseling and consulting are methods of helping people find alternatives and solutions and of guiding them through decision processes in which they can choose a suitable course of action. Providing answers can be disinviting because such behavior may signal a belief that the person is incapable of making appropriate decisions.

12. *Keep the volcano from erupting* By being accessible and keeping your eyes and ears open you will have the advantage of sensing when difficulties are approaching. This will enable you to be better prepared to offer help when it is needed. Even more important, it may allow you to use preventive strategies to avoid oncoming problems. The professionally inviting counselor handles little problems before they have a chance to become big ones.

13. *Keep the faith* It is important that the professional not lose heart in the face of rejection. If an invitation is sent it may or may not be accepted, but if it is not sent then it cannot be accepted. For this and other reasons, be not dismayed, and keep on inviting.

14. *Spread the word* How about a weekly column in your local newspaper to highlight school activities, special accomplishments, educational ideas, and innovations, and to educate the public generally about the many good things taking place in school.

15. *Invest a penny* "A penny for your thoughts." Tape a brand-new shiny penny to a small card and send one to each teacher in the school. On the card ask the teachers for their suggestions on how the counseling center and personnel can be of special assistance to them.

16. *Offer extra help* Many faculty and staff perform tasks that are above and beyond their usual responsibility. Often these jobs are done because the school cannot afford "extra" services. Lend a hand if you can possibly spare the time. Get down on the floor and paint some posters, hang decorations, chaperone field trips, sweep floors, make some educational games, or do whatever you can to invite a feeling of mutual professional support in your school.

17. *Hold a happy hour* Open up your center occasionally after school for teachers and others to enjoy refreshments and conversation. If space is limited, go to a larger room. This hour can be an excellent opportunity for the staff to develop a feeling of community as well as a time to present a minisession of new ideas. These gatherings may be for relaxing, with no business, or they may combine pleasure with some professionally interesting idea.

18. *Include the leadership*   Principals, supervisors, school board members, and others appreciate being invited to the counseling center for activities or events. This builds personal relationships between counselors and other professionals and also allows you to show off the counseling program and guidance activities in your school.

19. *Be accessible*   As a professional person in the school you provide important services. If you set up office hours that are an imposition to other people, then few people will feel welcome to use counseling services. Also, if you put the Do Not Disturb sign on your office door, expect people to become disturbed! Availability is a hallmark of the professionally inviting counselor.

20. *Be visible*   Visibility is an important part of accessibility. You may benefit by being out of your office as much as you are in it. Eat with students in the cafeteria, walk the halls during passing periods, and say hello to the teacher whose room is at the far end of the hall. This may be difficult if you are a secondary-school counselor, but it is important to be visible.

21. *Follow up*   If someone comes to you with a problem or shares something of a personal nature, be sure to ask about it later. This can be done formally or informally, and takes very little time. The important thing is to express your continued concern and interest.

22. *Strangle the paper monster*   Unfortunately, counselors are sometimes among those who create forms for teachers and students to fill out. Try to keep the methods of communication between you and your fellow professionals and students as easy and simple as possible. Time is precious. It should be valued highly and not spent on relatively unimportant paperwork.

23. *Improve your sign language*   Look at every sign and written communication posted in your counseling center and school. Are they inviting? For example, Office Closed, Do Not Disturb, or Do Not Take Records Out could be reworded so they convey the message while maintaining warmth and concern. Signs are to give directions; they should be positively worded and courteously stated. Please and Thank You should appear on every directive sign.

24. *Have a yearly review*   At the end of each school year ask all faculty and staff members to note down what they thought went well with the counseling program during the year, and where improvements might be made. When this is done in a positive manner, many good ideas can be generated for the coming year.

25. *Hold an open house at the end of the year*   Let friends of education know of your successes by holding an informal open house

toward the end of the school year. This provides a special opportunity to inform people about the many good things that were accomplished during the school year.

What School Secretaries Can Do

1. *Keep people posted* Ensure prompt and accurate communication in your school by using announcements, newsletters, flyers, and bulletin boards to keep everyone informed. Even a small blackboard near the mailboxes can be used to remind people of upcoming events. Use more than one system of communication to reach your audience.

2. *Organize student guides* Visitors to the school should be met quickly and cordially. Student guides are particularly helpful if the school has many visitors; they can serve as hosts and hostesses. Escorting parents, substitutes, and other visitors to the places they wish to be and helping them with their needs sets an inviting tone.

3. *Embrace the new teacher* While the administration usually acquaints new teachers with policies, experienced secretaries can also meet with new teachers to give them a survival manual of practical suggestions and words of comfort to help make their lives more enjoyable during that first year.

4. *Prepare some tooth fairy envelopes* If you work in an elementary school, have a special tooth fairy envelope ready for sending home that tooth that comes out at school. A clever little poem signed by the teacher and principal makes a special notice of a tender little moment in the life of a family.

5. *Plan comfortable meetings* A careful check of facilities before an activity begins helps to ensure that personal needs are met. These areas include seating, lighting, temperature, materials, restroom facilities, and related items of comfort. People participate best when they feel cared for.

6. *Install a student telephone* Providing a small convenience for students, such as a centrally located telephone that does not require permission to be used, is a special way to invite students to see themselves as able, valuable, and responsible. The phone can be programmed to take only local calls. Installing a student phone is worth the fairly small cost, as it reflects respect for students. When students are treated with respect, they are more likely to *show* respect.

7. *Share a phone* School telephones are sometimes protected as though they were a symbol of power. In many schools, teachers and other professionals do not have access to a private phone, yet they often need

one. By making your office phone available to others during appropriate times, you demonstrate an effort to develop a cooperative and caring relationship with your colleagues.

8. *Be prompt and patient*   Promptness and patience in listening are two important qualities of the school secretary. When callers and visitors are listened to patiently and attentively, they are in a much better position to express their needs and concerns, particularly when their presence in the office has been acknowledged promptly and courteously.

9. *Be professionally responsible*   An important way to improve the quality of life in your school is to be ethical in your conduct. Be trustworthy with confidences, follow rules (and if they are bad rules, work to change them), and support your colleagues and the purposes of your school.

10. *Stifle the public address system*   Along with discipline problems, disruptions rank among the biggest frustrations of teachers. Because interruptions can be most disinviting, the use of the public address system should be severely limited. Use of the PA system should be restricted to the first five, or last five, minutes of the learning period. (When the PA is used for announcements, it can also be used for happy messages such as a birthday announcement or the arrival of a new brother or sister.)

11. *Send double-strength compliments*   As nice as it is to receive kind words directly, it is even nicer to learn that kind words about you have been expressed to others. Rather than praising a student directly, praising the student to teachers, parents, or other students (when done sensitively) can be highly effective. The original praise will reach the person with double impact!

12. *Let people know you care*   When someone is ill or misses school for other reasons, a note or postcard can do wonders. Such a message need be nothing more than a sheet of paper containing a cheery note.

13. *Have your name known*   By either wearing a name tag or having a name plaque on your desk, you invite people to speak to a person rather than a position.

14. *Keep the office alive*   A bright and cheerful office offers a pleasant, nonverbal message about the quality of life in a school. Offices can be made more attractive by hanging live plants and having up-to-date reading materials available.

15. *Be a booster*   Attend school events, such as plays, interscholastic and intramural sports, and PTA meetings. Buy some band candy, purchase a yearbook, or donate some time to the school bazaar. Demonstrate your school spirit, and encourage students to do the same!

16. *Signal your handle* Encourage each person on the school staff and faculty to call you by the same name. It may be disinviting to some teachers if a few call you "Bob" while others address you as "Mr. Jones." Most people want to call you by the name you prefer, so let them know your preference.

17. *Be a craftsperson* Take pride in every letter or announcement that passes through your hands. Check carefully for spelling, syntax, and grammar. Every communication that goes out from the school represents the school and everyone in it.

18. *Share your attention* It is important to be accessible to the public, staff, and students. Although some priorities require more of your time, it is essential to let others know when you or someone else will be able to assist them.

19. *Rehearse the future, not the past* So often when we make a mistake, we go over it again and again in our minds—in effect, *practicing* the mistake. A better way of handling things is to ask: "How will I handle this problem next time?" By concentrating on future response behavior, we can rehearse the future, not the past.

20. *Follow through promptly* One of the most significant characteristics of the professionally inviting secretary is that he or she follows through promptly. The most positive action, when long delayed, loses much of its reward value.

21. *Make the telephone your ally* Most contacts with the school are by telephone and so it is important to be professional, personal, and positive. By answering the phone "Good morning, Jefferson High School, Ms. Bradley speaking" you accomplish all three. Saying "I don't know where the principal is; he hasn't been here all day" could be better stated: "The principal is out of the office at the moment, but may I help?" Another example: "You'll have to call back" might be replaced with "The principal is in a meeting. May I have your number so she may call you back as soon as the meeting is over?" Convey the message that the caller is important.

22. *Promote positive public relations* It's never a matter of whether or not the school has public relations, it's a matter of what kind! To promote positive public relations, make sure that the large majority of messages are stated affirmatively and clearly.

23. *Use the pinking shears* Pinking shears can be used to cut out some of the more beautiful pictures and messages written on the holiday cards you receive. These pictures and messages can be used to decorate an office for all occasions.

24. *Distribute resources efficiently and fairly* Efficient resource allocation is essential to success. Moreover, it is something over which the

secretary has direct control. Be as fair-minded as possible in providing material support to faculty and staff.

25. *Know your stuff* Finding, organizing, and sharing with proper authorities all the information needed to run a school is an important way in which secretaries are professionally inviting. Careful record-keeping and office organization benefits everyone in the school.

What Secondary-School Teachers Can Do

1. *Express your pleasure* At the beginning of the term, why not tell your students how pleased and honored your are to share their company during the semester? The students may never have heard this from a teacher before. It will bowl them over, and you are off to a good school year.

2. *Develop class spirit* Early in the school year the teacher can invite the class to decide upon a name for the group. The class might also select an emblem, motto, and class colors. These can be used on the outside of the classroom door, for classroom displays, and on messages to parents and students. By using many of the same techniques as athletic teams, a class can develop team spirit.

3. *Share names* A way to reduce threat at the beginning of the year is to encourage students to learn more about each other. To do this the teacher may ask students to tell the others in the group about their name. For example: "For whom were you named?" "What does your name mean?" "Does your name seem to fit you?" "Do you like your name?" "Have you ever been kidded about your name or had it mispronounced?" "What do you like to be called?" This simple ice-breaker invites students to talk about themselves in a nonthreatening manner. Also, it is likely to be of interest to students if they are encouraged to look up the etymology of their names in reference books.

4. *Invite dialogue* Explain to students that "It's not the answers to my questions that are important, it's the *questions* you have for my *answers.*" Knowledge is constantly unfolding, and today's accepted fact may soon become tomorrow's outmoded concept. By challenging ideas, students grow intellectually.

5. *Hold contests* For a few minutes (at the beginning or end of a class session) hold a contest to loosen things up. For example, a contest for the most terrible pun or most trivial trivia can invite a warm and friendly class feeling.

6. *Be with it* Make an effort to understand the world in which the student of today lives. For example, try to keep up with fads, fashions,

popular heroes, latest films, sports, TV programs, actors, singers, and other current interests of students. Using an instance from some TV program to invite learning of some academic concept can be quite effective.

7. *Tap expertise*   Your school cafeteria worker may be a classical music bug, the bus driver an amateur artist, the school psychologist or nurse a rock collector, the principal a woodworker, your fellow teacher a ballet dancer. Find the talents of people in school and invite them into your class to share their interests and lives with students.

8. *Rearrange space*   No matter how attractive, your room decorations and layout get stale. Change things around periodically, and be sure to ask those who share your space to assist in the planning and rearranging.

9. *Use the opaque*   An underutilized audiovisual aid in most schools is the opaque projector. With this simple machine you can reproduce almost any drawing or photograph in almost any larger size. You can fill an entire wall with a map of Europe, or show how a bill goes through Congress. Any drawing, with an opaque projector, large white paper, and students with magic markers who trace the projected drawing, can brighten the learning environment.

10. *Encourage participation*   When some students are not participating, it helps to divide and subdivide the class. Start out with pairs, then groups of four, later groups of eight and sixteen. It is difficult to remain silent when you are 50 percent of a group!

11. *Maintain a giveaway library*   Books are meant to be used and enjoyed. A way to encourage reading is for the teacher to read an occasional passage or brief section from a favorite book, then present the book to some student *as a gift*. Teachers may keep a fresh stock of books on hand by visiting garage sales, flea markets, and Goodwill Industries shops. It is worth the small cost for a student to hear a teacher say, "Here's a book I want you to have and enjoy. I think it was written just for you!"

12. *Collect junk*   While looking for books at flea markets and garage sales also look for objects that can be taken apart, put back together, manipulated—things like broken typewriters, clocks, and simple mechanical devices. Puzzles, toys, and gadgets can all be used to encourage imagination, develop simulation games, and invite learning. These activities have the potential for encouraging learning while inviting positive changes in self-concept.

13. *Make and take*   An unusual invitation is one that involves the production of something. A California teacher has students invest in the stock market and share results. Another teacher in Florida introduces students to geometry by making pancakes and dividing them in various ways. One student exclaimed after class, "Boy this was the best math lesson I ever ate."

14. *Share duties* There are many small tasks that students can do for the teacher. For example, taking roll, distributing and collecting materials, preparing experiments, even evaluation of work can involve students and make the life of teachers a little easier.

15. *Ask "What would you like to learn to do?"* Ask students this question on a short survey form. Where possible, plan and conduct mini-course electives for once-a-week sessions to meet the indicated interests. Learning Oriental cooking, studying photography, or attending a seminar on a special topic can be an excellent entree to English essays or mathematical problem solving. These special interest programs would be supplementary and supportive to well-designed academic courses and programs.

16. *Arrange a "big pal" program* Tutoring and related activities seem to help both the tutor and the one being tutored. Therefore, arrange a program where high-school students are matched with students from lower grades to offer support, assistance, and friendship.

17. *Open-end your questions* By asking questions that require more than a yes-or-no answer, the teacher invites discussion and dialogue. For example, "What do you think about. . . " and "How would you describe . . . " generate thinking and involvement.

18. *Now a word from our sponsor* Divide the class into small film companies and ask each company to prepare a one-minute commercial on an academic concept. Each company is invited to write, direct, and videotape their commercial for class viewing. This process gives both academic learning and class enthusiasm. It also encourages creativity.

19. *Organize an emergency packet* When you are faced with a no-good or very disinviting day, have an emergency packet ready that contains a few sure-fire lesson plans and enjoyable materials. It can save your sanity one day.

20. *Share your person* Let the students know that you have many dimensions other than just teacher. Share anecdotes about your family or pets. Let students know your feelings about books or movies, even share your moods. You will be surprised at how thoughtful and caring students can be when you tell them you have a headache and "please be gentle with me."

21. *Involve students in decisions* If your system is one in which teachers select textbooks, ask students of varying backgrounds and achievement to help preview textbooks before decisions are made. After all, who knows better than students which books are inviting? Students can also participate in the decision-making process in other areas, such as rules of conduct, academic expectations, and even teacher selection!

22.   *Use a Zen koan*   Zen masters use koans to invite their students to reflect deeply on one's self and one's relation to the world. A koan is a simple question that has no simple answer. It is the student's struggle with the koan, not the teaching of the master, that enlightens the student.

23.   *Be the greeter, be the leave-taker*   At the beginning and end of each class session, take a minute or two to establish a caring environment. Share a thought, talk about a current event, ask about things; let students know we are human beings first, and teachers or students second.

24.   *Use collective, inclusive pronouns*   Using such pronouns as *we, us,* and *our* in class seems to be more inviting than using *you* or *yours.* For example, a teacher says: *We've* got to get *our* work done so *we* can move along." This seems preferable to: "*You* students must get *your* work done." Using the collective term invites a feeling of family.

25.   *Change color*   If you use red ink or pencil to grade papers, perhaps it is time to switch to a felt-tip marker, highlighter, or to any color other than red. The color red has negative connotations to many students.

INVITING AND DISINVITING SIGNALS

The following lists of inviting and disinviting verbal comments, personal behaviors, physical environments, and printed signs have been identified by educators and students as indicators of the quality of life in schools. These lists are only illustrative, but the presence or absence of items on these lists may help to identify the inviting or disinviting stance taken by those who live and work in and around schools. These items may also serve as a checklist for those in schools who are already doing good things, and who want to do them even better.

Verbal Comments

Forty Inviting Comments
Good morning.
Thanks very much.
Congratulations.
Let's talk it over.
How can I help?
Tell me about it.
I appreciate your help.
Happy birthday!
I enjoy having you here.
I understand.
We missed you.
I'm glad you came by.
I like that idea!
I think you can.
Welcome.
I like what you did.
Welcome back.
You are unique.
That's even better.
I've been thinking about you.
How are things going?
How are you?
I'd like your opinion.
Happy holiday!
What do you think?
Let's have lunch.
What can I do for you?
Of course I have time.
That's OK.
I am impressed!
You made me feel good.
Yes.
Please come in.
I've always got time for you.
I think you can do it.
Please tell me more.
May I help you?
Let's do it together.
Come back soon!
I enjoy our time together.

Forty Disinviting Comments
Keep out.
What Mary is trying to say is . . .
Use your head.
It won't work.
You'll have to call back.
You can't do that.
I don't care what you do.
Not bad, for a girl.
Don't be so stupid.
Who do you think you are?
He can't be disturbed.
Why didn't you stay at home?
Woman driver.
They don't want to learn.
They don't have the ability.
You can't be that dumb.
They're all right, in their place.
Who's calling?
You should not feel that way.
You ought to know better.
You must do as I say.
How could you?
Shape up or ship out.
Anybody can do that.
Why do you bother coming to school?
That's a childish viewpoint.
That is dead wrong.
Hi, Chubby.
You goofed.
Get lost.
That's stupid.
So what?
Because I said so, that's why.
What, you again?
Forget it.
You'll never make it.
Sit down and shut up.
Knock it off.
I know you're not that stupid.
What's your excuse this time?

Personal Behaviors

Forty Inviting Behaviors
A relaxed posture
Lending a book
Smiling
Listening carefully
Patting a back
Shaking hands
Opening a door for someone
Giving a friendly wink
Sharing lunch together
Being on time
Sending a thoughtful note
Bringing a gift
Sharing an experience
Accepting praise
Giving wait-time
Gazing warmly
Yielding interest
Noticing new clothes
Learning names
Offering refreshments
Sending a valentine
Hugging (where appropriate)
Extending an apology (where
  required)
Picking up litter
Planting a flower
Waiting your turn
Holding a door
Extending a hand
Congratulating someone
Sharing a poem
Remembering important occasions
Sharing a sandwich
Using a napkin
Offering someone a chair
Bringing flowers
Scratching someone's back
Expressing regret
Waving with both hands
Giving a thumbs-up sign
Overlooking a faux pas

Forty Disinviting Behaviors
Giving a thumbs-down sign
Interrupting
Looking at your watch
Yawning in someone's face
Shaking your finger at someone
Scowling and frowning
Slamming a door
Using ridicule
Turning your back on someone
Cutting people short
Making fun of a person
Looking away from someone
Leaving someone to answer the
  phone
Hitting someone
Being obscene
Laughing at someone's misfortune
Throwing paper on ground
Tapping a pencil (fidgeting)
Chewing gum loudly
Breaking a promise
Forgetting an important date
Gawking at an accident
Using sarcasm
Mimicking
Forgetting a birthday
Blowing your car horn
Talking with your mouth full
Playing with your nose
Eating loudly
Showing lack of concern
Sneering
Being late
Staring at someone
Littering
Shoving ahead
Stamping your foot
Telling a lie
Dumping ashtrays in the street
Insulting a person
Talking during a movie

Physical Environments

Forty Inviting Qualities
Fresh paint
Pleasant smells
Living plant
Attractive, up-to-date bulletin boards
Soft lighting
Big and soft pillows
Lots of books
Fresh air
Fireplace
Comfortable furniture
Rocking chair
Flowers on the desk
Open doors
Candy jar with candy
Soft music
Attractive pictures
Comfortable temperature
A cup of coffee, tea, or juice
Porch light at night
Porch swing
Birthday cake
Fresh towels
Well-tended park
Books and magazines
Stuffed animals
Sunny room
Game board
Thick carpet
This morning's paper
Holiday tree
Matching colors
Birthday card
Positively worded signs
Blue jeans and cotton shirts
Bright hallways
Clean aromas
Brightly lit parking lot
Clean windows
Clear floors
Old pick-up truck

Forty Disinviting Qualities
Dark corridors
Bad smells
Dingy colors
Full trash cans
Hard lighting
Insects (flies, roaches)
Excessive noise
Smoke-filled room
Bare walls
Leftover food
Dirty coffee cups
Full ashtrays
Bare lightbulb
Stack of out-of-date materials
Fluorescent lights that buzz
Dark parking lots
A full pencil sharpener
Dead plant
Long line
Dingy curtains
Burned-out lightbulbs
Sidewalks going where people don't
Opaque windows
Cold room
Lukewarm coffee
Artificial plants and flowers
Cigarette butts on a plate
Sink full of dirty dishes
Exhaust fumes
Straight rows
Empty mail box
Dirty fingerprints
Peeling paint and plaster
Nothing to read
Dusty, cobwebby shelves
Stuffy room
Sticky floors
Broken windows
Signs with letters missing
Spray-painted graffiti

Printed Signs

Forty Inviting Signs	*Forty Disinviting Signs*
Please Use Sidewalks	Office Closed
Welcome	Do Not Disturb
Visitor Parking	Keep off Grass
Please Leave Message	No Trespassing
Open, Come In	No Talking
No Appointment Necessary	No Running in Halls
Please Use Other Door	No Admission without Pass
Thank You for Not Smoking	No Admittance
Come Back Soon	Visitors Must Report to _____
Open House	No Smoking
We're Glad You're Here	Be Seated
Handicapped Parking	Keep Out
Sorry I Missed You, Please Come Back	Do Not Enter
	No Deposit, No Return
Visitors Welcome	Tow Zone
Happy Hour	By Appointment Only
Please Put Litter Here	Out of Order
Come As You Are	Beware of the Dog
Open to the Public	No Children Allowed
Rest Area	Closed to the Public
Take Me	Private Beach
Clean Restrooms	No Checks Cashed
Help Keep North Carolina Beautiful	No Spitting on Sidewalk
	Members Only
Library	For Faculty Use Only
Have Lunch with Us	We Do Not Give Change
Students Welcome Back	Take a Number and Wait
Please Excuse the Inconvience	Shoplifters Will Be Prosecuted: This Means You!
Good Day	
Happy Holidays	Keep This Door *Shut!*
No Waiting	Stay in Line
You're Here	Not for Public Use
Please Touch	Out to Lunch
Come on In	You Broke It, You Bought It
Pardon Our Dust	Books Are for Sale Only
Ample Parking in the Rear	Government Property—No Admittance
May We Help You?	
Be Back at _____	Do Not Remove under Penalty of Law
Please Watch Your Step	Restrooms for Customers Only
Help Us Conserve Energy	Parking for Officials Only
Directory Assistance	No Shirt, No Service
Welcome to Canada	No Facilities

REFERENCES

Alberti, R. E., and Emmons, M. L. *Your perfect right: A guide to assertive behavior* (2nd ed.). San Luis Obispo, Calif.: Impact, 1974.

Allport, G. W. *Personality: A psychological interpretation.* New York: Holt, Rinehart & Winston, 1937.

Allport, G. W. The ego in contemporary psychology. *Psychological Review,* 1943, *50,* 451–478.

Allport, G. W. *Becoming.* New Haven: Yale University Press, 1955.

Allport, G. W. *Pattern and growth in personality.* New York: Holt, Rinehart & Winston, 1961.

Aronson, E., and Carlsmith, J. M. Performance expectancy as a determinant of actual performance. *Journal of Abnormal and Social Psychology,* 1962, *65,* 178–182.

Aspy, D. N., and Buhler, J. H. The effect of teachers' inferred self-concept upon student achievement. *Journal of Educational Research,* 1975, *47,* 386–389.

Avila, D., and Purkey, W. Intrinsic and extrinsic motivation: A regrettable distinction. *Psychology in the Schools,* 1966, *3,* 206–210.

Bachman, J. G., and O'Malley, P. M. Self-esteem in young men: A longitudinal analysis of the impact of educational and occupational attainment. *Journal of Personality and Social Psychology,* 1977, *35,* 365–380.

Baker, J. P., and Crist, J. L. Teacher expectancies: A review of the literature. In J. D. Elashoff and R. E. Snow (Eds.), *Pygmalion reconsidered.* Worthington, Ohio: Charles A. Jones, 1971.

Bellack, A., Kliebard, H., Hyman, R., and Smith, F. *The language of the classroom.* New York: Teachers' College Press, 1966.

Bennett, A. C., and Novak, J. M. *Looking for the inviting and just school environment.* Paper presented at the meeting of the American Educational Research Association, Los Angeles, April 1981.

Bennett, J. *Regrets and prides: Invitations accepted or not accepted.* Unpublished paper, University of North Carolina at Greensboro, 1982.

Berger, P., and Luckman, T. *The social construction of reality: A treatise in the sociology of knowledge.* Garden City, N.Y.: Doubleday, 1966.

Bloom, B. S. *Human characteristics and school learning.* New York: McGraw-Hill, 1976.

Bloom, B. S. The new direction in educational research: Alterable variables. *Phi Delta Kappan,* 1980, *61,* 382–385.

Bogdan, R. C., and Biklen, S. K. *Qualitative research for education: An introduction to theory and methods.* Boston: Allyn & Bacon, 1982.

Bogdan, R. C., and Taylor, S. The judged, not the judges: An insider's view of mental retardation. *American Psychologist,* 1976, *31,* 47–52.

Branch, C. *An investigation of inferred and professed self-concept-as-learner of disruptive and nondisruptive middle school students.* Unpublished doctoral dissertation, University of Florida, 1974.

Branch, C., Damico, S., and Purkey, W. A comparison between the self-concepts as learner of disruptive and nondistruptive middle school students. *The Middle School Journal,* 1977, *7,* 15–16.

Braun, C. Teacher expectation: Sociopsychological dynamics. *Review of Educational Research,* 1976, *42*(2), 185–213.

Brophy, J. E. *Teacher behaviors related to learning by low vs. high socio-economic status early elementary students.* Paper presented at the meeting of the American Educational Research Association, Washington, D.C., April 1975.

Brophy, J. E. Teacher behavior and its effects. *Journal of Educational Psychology,* 1979, *71*(6), 733–750.

Brophy, J. E., and Evertson, C. M. *Learning from teaching: A developmental perspective.* Boston: Allyn & Bacon, 1976.

Brophy, J. E., and Good, T. L. *Teacher–student relationships: Causes and consequences.* New York: Holt, Rinehart & Winston, 1974.

Brown, C. *Manchild in the promised land.* New York: Macmillan, 1965.

Brubaker, D. L. *Creative leadership in elementary schools.* Dubuque: Kendall/Hunt, 1976.

Bruner, J. S. *The process of education.* Cambridge, Mass.: Harvard University Press, 1960.

Buber, M. *The knowledge of man: Selected essays.* New York: Harper & Row, 1965.

Bugelski, B. R. *The psychology of learning applied to teaching* (Rev. ed.). New York: Bobbs-Merrill, 1971.

Campbell, J. R. *Pattern analysis—A macroscopic development for interaction analysis.* Paper presented at the meeting of the National Association for Research in Science Teaching, Chicago, March 1973.

Canfield, J., and Wells, H. *100 Ways to enhance self-concept in the classroom: A handbook for teachers and parents.* Englewood Cliffs, N.J.: Prentice-Hall, 1976.

Carnoy, M. (Ed.). *Schooling in a corporate society.* New York: David McKay, 1972.

Carroll, L. *Alice in wonderland.* New York: W. W. Norton, 1971.

Cartwright, D. S., Tomson, B., and Schwartz, H. (Eds.). *Gang delinquency.* Monterey, Calif.: Brooks/Cole, 1975.

Chaikin, A. L., and Sigler, E. *Non-verbal mediators of teacher expectancy effects.* Paper presented at the annual meeting of the Eastern Psychological Association, Washington, D.C., 1973.

Chamberlin, J. G. *The educating act: A phenomenological view.* Washington, D.C.: University Press of America, 1981.

Charles, C. M. *Building classroom discipline: From models to practice.* New York: Longman, 1981.

Child, I. L. *Humanistic psychology and the research tradition: Their several virtues.* New York: John Wiley, 1973.

Children's Defense Fund of the Washington Research Project, *Children out of School in America.* Cambridge, Mass.: Author, 1975.

Childs, J. L. *Education and the philosophy of experimentalism.* New York: Century, 1931.

Clark, D. H. *Social therapy in psychiatry.* Baltimore, Md.: Penguin Books, 1974.

Coleman, J. S. *Equality of educational opportunity* (Department of Health, Education, and Welfare). Washington, D.C.: U.S. Government Printing Office, 1966.

Combs, A. W. (Ed.). *Perceiving, behaving, becoming.* Washington, D.C.: Yearbook of the Association for Supervision and Curriculum Development, 1962.

Combs, A. W. Some basic concepts for teacher education. *The Journal of Teacher Education,* 1972, *23,* 286–290.

Combs, A. W. *A personal approach to teaching: Beliefs that make a difference.* Boston: Allyn & Bacon, 1982.

Combs, A. W., Avila, D., and Purkey, W. W. *Helping relationships: Basic concepts for the helping professions* (2nd ed.). Boston: Allyn & Bacon, 1978.

Combs, A. W., Blume, R. A., Newman, A. J., and Wass, H. L. *The professional education of teachers: A humanistic approach to teacher preparation* (2nd ed.). Boston: Allyn & Bacon, 1974.

Combs, A. W., Richards, A. C., and Richards, F. *Perceptual psychology: A humanistic approach to the study of persons.* New York: Harper & Row, 1976.

Combs, A. W., and Snygg, D. *Individual behavior: A perceptual approach to behavior* (2nd ed.). New York: Harper & Row, 1959.

Combs, A. W., Soper, D. W., Gooding, C. T., Benton, J. A., Jr., Dickman, J. F., and Usher, R. H. *Florida studies in the helping professions* (Social Science Monograph No. 37). Gainesville, Fla.: University of Florida Press, 1969.

Coopersmith, S. *The antecedents of self-esteem.* San Francisco: W. H. Freeman, 1967.

Cormany, R. B. *Guidance and counseling in Pennsylvania: Status and needs.* Lemoyne, Pa.: ESEA Title III Project, West Shore School District, 1975.

Cotler, S. B., and Guerra, J. J. *Assertion training: A humanistic behavioral guide to self-dignity.* Champaign, Ill.: Research Press, 1976.

Coudert, J. *Advice from a failure.* New York: Dell, 1965.

Cousins, N. Editorial. *Saturday Review,* January 23, 1971, p. 31.

Curtis, J., and Altman, H. The relationship between teachers' self-concept and self-concept of students. *Child Study Journal,* 1977, 7(1), 17–26.

Curtis, R. C., Zanna, M. P., and Campbell, W. W. Sex, fear of success and the perceptions and performance of law school students. *American Educational Research Journal,* 1975, *12*(3), 287–297.

Damico, S. *Education by peers: A clique study* (Research Monograph No. 9). P. K. Yonge Laboratory School, University of Florida, August 1974.

Damico, S. Clique membership and its relationship to academic achievement and attitude toward school. *Journal of Research and Development in Education,* 1976, 9(4), 29–35.

DeCharms, R. *Personal causation: The internal affective determinants of behavior.* New York: Academic Press, 1968.

DeCharms, R. Personal-causation training in schools. *Journal of Applied Social Psychology,* 1972, *2,* 95–113.

Derlega, V. J., and Chaikin, A. L. *Sharing intimacy: What we reveal to others and why.* Englewood Cliffs, N.J.: Prentice-Hall, 1975.

Deutsch, M. The disadvantaged child and the learning process. In A. H. Passow (Ed.), *Education in depressed areas.* New York: Bureau of Publications, Teachers' College, Columbia University, 1963.

Dewey, J. *Democracy and education.* New York: Macmillan, 1916.

Dewey, J. *How we think.* Lexington, Mass.: D. C. Heath, 1933.

Diggory, J. C. *Self-evaluation: Concepts and studies.* New York: John Wiley, 1966.

Dollar, B. *Humanizing classroom discipline: A behavioral approach.* New York: Harper & Row, 1972.

Dorland's Illustrated Medical Dictionary (25th ed.). Philadelphia: W. B. Saunders, 1974.

Dowaliby, F. J., and Schumer, H. Teacher-centered versus student-centered mode of college instruction as related to manifest anxiety. *Journal of Educational Psychology,* 1973, *64,* 125–132.

Doyle, W., Hancock, G., and Kifer, E. Teachers' perceptions: Do they make a difference? *Journal of the Association for the Study of Perception,* 1972, *7,* 21–30.

Dreikurs, R., and Cassel, P. *Discipline without tears.* New York: Hawthorne, 1974.

Drugger, C. W. *The relationship between expressed acceptance of self, expressed acceptance of others and supervising teachers' predictions of student teachers' probable success in teaching.* Unpublished doctoral disseration, University of Oregon, 1971.

Dumas, A. *The three musketeers.* New York: Macmillan, 1962. (Originally published, 1844.)

Edelwich, J. (with Brodsky, A.). *Burnout: Stages of disillusionment in the helping professions.* New York: Human Sciences Press, 1980.

Egan, G. *The skilled helper: A model for systematic helping and interpersonal relating.* Monterey, Calif.: Brooks/Cole, 1975.

Elkind, D. *The hurried child: Growing up too fast too soon.* Reading, Mass.: Addison-Wesley, 1981.

Epstein, J. L., and McPartland, J. M. The concept and measurement of the quality of school life. *American Educational Research Journal,* 1976, *13*(1), 15–30.

Epstein, S. The self-concept revisited: Or theory of a theory. *American Psychologist,* May 1973, 404–415.

Farina, A. *Abnormal psychology.* Englewood Cliffs, N.J.: Prentice-Hall, 1976.

Felice, L. G. *Self-concept: The linkage between family background, school context and educational success.* Paper presented at the meeting of the American Educational Research Association, Washington, D.C., March 1975.

Felker, E. W. *Building positive self-concepts.* Minneapolis: Burgess, 1974.

Fielder, W. R., Cohen, R. D., and Finney, S. An attempt to replicate the teacher expectancy effect. *Psychological Reports,* 1971, *29,* 1223–1228.

Findley, W., and Bryan, M. *The pros and cons of ability grouping. Fastback 66.* Bloomington, Ind.: Phi Delta Kappa Educational Foundation, 1975.

Fisher, R., and Ury, W. *Getting to yes: Negotiating agreement without giving in.* Boston: Houghton Mifflin, 1981.

Fitts, W. H., and Hamner, W. T. *The self concept and delinquency* (Nashville Mental Health Center Monograph No. 1). Nashville, Tenn.: Counselor Recordings and Tests, 1969.

Frericks, A. H. *Labeling of students by prospective teachers.* Paper presented at the meeting of the American Educational Research Association, Chicago, March 1974.

Friedman, H., and Friedman, P. *Frequency and types of teacher reinforcement given to lower- and middle-class students.* Paper presented at the meeting of the American Educational Research Association, 1973.

Fromm, E. *Man for himself.* New York: Rinehart, 1947.

Garber, J., and Seligmann, M. (Eds.). *Human helplessness: Theory and applications.* New York: Academic Press, 1980.

Gaudry, E., and Spielberger, C. D. (Eds.). *Anxiety and educational achievement.* New York: John Wiley, 1971.

Gerber, T. *The young adolescent: Invitations to school success.* Paper presented at the meeting of the American Educational Research Association Convention, New York, March 1982.

Gergen, K. J. *The concept of self.* New York: Holt, Rinehart, & Winston, 1971.

Giorgi, A. *Psychology as a human science: A phenomenologically-based approach.* New York: Harper & Row, 1970.

Glock, M. D. Is there a Pygmalion in the classroom? *The Reading Teacher,* 1972, *25,* 405–408.

Goldberg, M. L. Studies in underachievement among the academically talented. In A. Frazier (Ed.), *Freeing capacity to learn.* Washington, D.C.: Fourth Association for Supervision and Curriculum Development (ASCD) Research Institute, 1960.

Good, T. L. Which pupils do teachers call on? *The Elementary School Journal,* 1970, *70,* 190–198.

Good, T. L. Teacher influence and student influence: A brief comment (Technical Report No. 221, Center for Research in Social Behavior). Columbia, Mo.: University of Missouri, 1980.

Good, T. L. Teacher expectations and student perceptions: A decade of research. *Educational Leadership,* 1981, *38*(5), 415–422.

Good, T. L., Biddle, B. J., and Brophy, J. E. *Teachers make a difference.* New York: Holt, Rinehart & Winston, 1975.

Good, T., and Brophy, J. *Educational psychology: A realistic approach.* New York: Holt, Rinehart & Winston, 1977.

Good, T., and Brophy, J. *Looking in classrooms* (2nd ed.). New York: Harper & Row, 1978.

Gordon, T. *T.E.T.: Teacher effectiveness training.* New York: Peter H. Wyden, 1974.

Grant, B. M., and Hennings, D. G. *The teacher moves: An analysis of non-verbal activity.* New York: Teachers College Press, 1971.

Graves, W. H. *A multivariate investigation of professed and inferred self concepts of fifth and sixth grade students.* Unpublished doctoral dissertation, University of Florida, 1972.

Gregory, D. *Nigger.* New York: Simon & Schuster, 1964.

Haan, R. F. *Accelerated learning programs.* New York: Center for Applied Research in Education, 1963.

Hall, E. T. *The silent language.* New York: Doubleday, 1959.

Hansen, J. C., and Maynard, P. E. *Youth: Self-concept and behavior.* Columbus, Ohio: Charles E. Merrill, 1973.

Haskins, J., and Butts, H. *The psychology of black language.* New York: Barnes & Noble, 1973.

Herbert, C. *I see a child.* New York: Anchor Books, 1974.

Hinde, R. A. (Ed.). *Non-verbal communication.* New York: Cambridge University Press, 1972.

Hobbs, N. *The futures of children.* San Francisco: Jossey-Bass, 1975. (a)

Hobbs, N. (Ed.). *The futures of children: Categories, labels, and their consequences.* Nashville, Tenn.: Vanderbilt University Press, 1975. (b)

Holmes, M., Holmes, D., and Field, J. *The therapeutic classroom.* New York: Aronson, 1974.

Hook, S. *John Dewey: An intellectual portrait.* New York: John Day, 1939.

House, P., and More, A. *The learning environment as a predictor of the academic self-concepts of ninth grade mathematics students.* Paper presented at the meeting of the American Educational Research Association, Chicago, March 1974.

Hunt, J. M. *Intelligence and experience.* New York: Ronald Press, 1961.

Inglis, S. C. *The development and validation of an instrument to assess teacher invitations and teacher effectiveness as reported by students in a technical and general post-secondary educational setting.* Unpublished doctoral dissertation, University of Florida, 1976.

Insel, P., and Jacobson, L. *What do you expect? An inquiry into self-fulfilling prophecies.* Menlo Park, Calif.: Cummings, 1975.

Irwin, F. S. Sentence-completion responses and scholastic success or failure. *Journal of Counseling Psychology,* 1967, *14,* 269–271.

Ivey, A. E. The intentional individual: A process–outcome view of behavioral psychology. *The Counseling Psychologist,* 1968, *1,* 56–59.

James, W. *Principles of psychology.* (2 vols.). New York: Henry Holt, 1890.

Jersild, A. T. *In search of self.* New York: Columbia University Press, 1952.

Jones, S. C., and Panitch, D. The self-fulfilling prophecy and interpersonal attraction. *Journal of Experimental Social Psychology,* 1971, *7,* 356–366.

Jourard, S. M. *The transparent self: Self-disclosure and well-being.* Princeton, N.J.: Van Nostrand, 1964.

Jourard, S. M. (Ed.). *To be or not to be: Existential psychological perspectives on the self.* Tallahassee: Board of Commissioners of State Institutions of Florida, 1967.

Jourard, S. M. *Disclosing man to himself.* Princeton, N.J.: Van Nostrand, 1968.

Jourard, S. M. *Self disclosure: An experimental analysis of the transparent self.* New York: Wiley–Interscience, 1971.

Joyce, B., and Weil, M. *Models of teaching* (2nd ed.). Englewood Cliffs, N.J.: Prentice-Hall, 1980.

Kegan, R. *The evolving self: Problem and process in human development.* Cambridge, Mass.: Harvard University Press, 1982.

Kelley, H. H. The process of causal attribution. *American Psychologist,* 1973, *28,* 107–128.

Kelly, G. A. *The psychology of personal constructs* (Vols. 1 & 2). New York: W. W. Norton, 1955.

Kelly, G. A. *Theory of personality: The psychology of personal constructs.* New York: Norton Library, 1963.

Kesey, K. *One flew over the cuckoo's nest.* New York: Viking Press, 1962.

Knowles, J. H. The responsibility of the individual. In J. H. Knowles (Ed.), *Doing better and feeling worse: Health in the United States.* New York: W. W. Norton, 1977.

Koffman, R. G. *A comparison of the perceptual organization of outstanding and randomly selected teachers in open and traditional classrooms.* Unpublished doctoral dissertation, University of Massachusetts, 1975.

Kohlberg, L. Stage and sequence: The cognitive-developmental approach to socialization. In D. A. Goslin (Ed.), *Handbook of socialization theory and research.* Chicago: Rand-McNally, 1969.

Kohlberg, L., and Turiel, E. *Research in moral development: The cognitive-developmental approach.* New York: Holt, Rinehart & Winston, 1971.

Kraft, A. *The living classroom: Putting humanistic education into practice.* New York: Harper & Row, 1975.

Kranz, P. L., Weber, W. A., and Fishell, K. N. *The relationships between teacher perception of pupils and teacher behavior toward those pupils.* Paper presented at the meeting of the American Educational Research Association, Minneapolis, March 1970.

Lambeth, C. R. *Teacher invitations and effectiveness as reported by secondary students in Virginia.* Unpublished doctoral dissertation, University of Virginia, 1980.

Landry, R. G. *Achievement and self concept: A curvilinear relationship.* Paper presented at the annual meeting of the American Educational Research Association, Chicago, 1974.

Landry, R. G., and Edeburn, C. E. *Teacher self-concept and student self-concept.* Paper presented at the American Educational Research Association, Chicago, April 1974.

Lasch, C. *The culture of narcissism: American life in an age of diminishing expectations.* New York: W. W. Norton, 1979.

Lecky, P. *Self-consistency: A theory of personality.* New York: Island Press, 1945.

Lee, H. *To kill a mockingbird.* Philadelphia: J. B. Lippincott, 1960.

Lefcourt, H. M. *Locus of control: Current trends in theory and research.* Hillsdale, N.J.: Erlbaum, 1976.

Lepper, M. R., and Greene, D. Turning play into work: Effects of adult surveillance and extrinsic rewards on childrens' intrinsic motivation. *Journal of Personality and Social Psychology,* 1975, *31,* 479–486.

Levin, D. *Soviet education today.* New York: John DeGraff, 1959.

Leviton, H., and Kiraly, J. Intervention strategies for promotions self-concept development. *Academic Therapy,* 1979, *14*(5), 535–545.

Liebman, J. L. *Peace of mind.* New York: Simon & Schuster, 1946.

Lifton, W. *Working with groups.* New York: John Wiley, 1962.

Lippitt, R., and White, R. *Autocracy and democracy.* New York: Harper, 1960.

Maehr, M. *Sociocultural origins of achievement.* Monterey, Calif.: Brooks/Cole, 1974.

Mahon, R., and Altman, H. Skill training: Cautions and recommendations. *Counselor Education and Supervision,* 1977, *17*(1), 42–50.

Mahoney, M. J. *Cognition and behavior modification.* Cambridge, Mass.: Ballinger, 1974.

Mahoney, M. J. The sensitive scientist in empirical humanism. *American Psychologist,* 1975, *30,* 864–867.

Manning, J. Discipline in the good old days. *Phi Delta Kappan,* 1959, *41*(3), 87–91.

Maslow, A. H. *Motivation and personality* (2nd ed.). New York: Harper & Row, 1970.

Masters, E. L. *Spoon River anthology.* New York: Macmillan, 1922.

May, R. *Love and will.* New York: W. W. Norton, 1969.

McDonald, F., and Elias, P. *The effects of teaching performance on pupil learning.* Vol. 1, Final Report, (Beginning Teacher Evaluation Study, Phase 2, 1974–1976). Princeton, N.J.: Educational Testing Service, 1976.

McLuhan, M., and Fiore, Q. *The medium is the massage.* New York: Random House, 1967.

Mead, G. H. *Mind self and society.* Chicago: University of Chicago Press, 1934.

Mehrabian, A. *Tactics of social influence.* Englewood Cliffs, N.J.: Prentice-Hall, 1970.

Mehrabian, A. *Nonverbal communication.* Chicago: Aldine-Atherton, 1972.

Mehrabian, A. *Silent messages* (2nd ed.). Belmont Calif.: Wadsworth, 1981.

Meichenbaum, D. *Cognitive behavior modification.* Morristown, N.J.: General Learning Press, 1974.

Mendels, G. E., and Flanders, J. P. Teachers' expectations and pupil performance. *American Educational Research Journal,* 1973, *10*(3), 203–212.

Mettee, D. R. Rejection of unexpected success as a function of the negative consequences of accepting success. *Journal of Personality and Social Psychology,* 1971, *17,* 332–341.

Mizer, J. E. Cipher in the snow. *NEA Journal,* 1964, *53,* 8–10.

Moore, T. W. *Educational theory: An introduction.* London: Routledge & Kegan Paul, 1974.

Moustakas, C. E. *The authentic teacher: Sensitivity and awareness in the classroom.* Cambridge, Mass.: Howard A. Doyle, 1966.

Niebuhr, R. Faith and history: A comparison of Christian and modern views of history. New York: Charles Scribner's, 1949.

Noad, B. M. Influence of self-concept and educational attitudes on elementary student teacher performance. *Educational Research Quarterly,* 1979, *4*(1), 69–75.

Notz, W. W. Work motivation and the negative effects of extrinsic rewards. A review with implications for theory and practice. *American Psychologist,* 1975, *30*(9), 884–891.

O'Roark, A. M. *A comparison of the perceptual characteristics of elected legislators and public school counselors identified as most and least effective.* Unpublished doctoral dissertation, University of Florida, 1974.

Owen, E. H. *A comparison of disadvantaged and non-disadvantaged elementary school pupils on two measures of self concept as learner.* Unpublished doctoral dissertation, University of Florida, 1972.

Patterson, C. H. The self in recent Rogerian theory. *Journal of Individual Psychology,* 1961, *17,* 5–11.

Patterson, C. H. *Humanistic education.* Englewood Cliffs, N.J.: Prentice-Hall, 1973.

Phares, E. J. *Locus of control in personality.* Morristown, N.J.: General Learning Press, 1976.

Pine, G. J., and Boy, A. V. Self-enrichment through teaching. *Clearinghouse,* 1979, *53,* 46–49.

Plum, A. Communication as skill: A critique and alternative proposal. *Journal of Humanistic Psychology,* 1981, *21*(4), 3–19.

Pomerance, B. *The Elephant man.* New York: Grove Press, 1979.

Powers, W. T. *Behavior: The control of perception.* Chicago: Aldine, 1973.

Pullias, E. V. *A common sense philosophy for modern man.* New York: Philosophical Library, 1975.

Purkey, W. W. *Self-concept and school achievement.* Englewood Cliffs, N.J.: Prentice Hall, 1970.

Purkey, W. W. The invitational secondary school. *Thresholds in Secondary Education,* 1975, *3,* 16–19.

Purkey, W. W. Invitations from Mr. Jefferson. *Proceedings, University of Virginia Education Day,* May 1976. (a)

Purkey, W. W. Powerful invitations in education. *Iowa Association for School, College, and University Newsletter.* Iowa City: University of Iowa, October 1976. (b)

Purkey, W. W., and Avila, D. L. Classroom discipline: A self concept approach. *Elementary School Journal,* 1971, *6,* 325–328.

Purkey, W. W., Cage, B., and Graves, W. The Florida Key: A scale to infer learner self concept. *Journal of Educational and Psychological Measurement,* 1973, *33,* 979–984.

Purkey, W.W., Graves, W., and Zellner, M. Self-perceptions of pupils in an experimental elementary school. *Elementary School Journal,* 1970, *71*(3), 166–171.

Raimy, V. C. Self-reference in counseling interviews. *Journal of Consulting Psychology,* 1948, *12,* 153–163.

Reis, R. Learning your students' names. *Education,* 1972, *93,* 45–46.

Richards, A. C., and Richards, F. *Goals of educational psychology in teacher education: A humanistic perspective.* Paper presented at the meeting of the American Educational Research Association, Washington, D.C., March 1975.

Riley, J. W. *James Whitcomb Riley's Complete Works* (Vol. 5). New York: Bobbs-Merrill, 1916.

Rist, R. C. Student social class and teacher expectations: The self fulfilling prophecy in ghetto education. *Harvard Educational Review,* 1970, *40,* 411–451.

Rogers, C. R. Some observations on the organization of personality. *American Psychologist,* 1947, *2,* 358–368.

Rogers, C. R. *Client-centered therapy.* Boston: Houghton Mifflin, 1951.

Rogers, C. R. *Counseling and psychotherapy: Theory and practice.* New York: Harper & Row, 1959.

Rogers, C. R. The therapeutic relationship: Recent theory and research. *Australian Journal of Psychology,* 1965, *17*(2), 95–108.

Rogers, C. R. *Coming into existence.* New York: World, 1967.

Rogers, C. R. *Freedom to learn.* Columbus, Ohio: Charles E. Merrill, 1969.

Rogers, C. R. My philosophy of interpersonal relationships and how it grew. *Journal of Humanistic Psychology,* 1973, *13*(2), 12–19.

Rogers, C. R. In retrospect—Forty-six years. *American Psychologist,* 1974, *29*(2), 115.

Rogers, C. R. The interpersonal relationship in the facilitation of learning. In R. R. Leeper (Ed.), *Humanizing education: The person in the process.* Washington, D.C.: Association for Supervision and Curriculum Development, 1976.

Rogers, C. R. *A way of being.* Boston: Houghton Mifflin, 1980.

Rosenberg, M. J. *Society and the adolescent self image.* Princeton, N.J.: Princeton University Press, 1965.

Rosenberg, M. J. Discussion: The concepts of self. In R. P. Abelson, E. Aronson, W. McGuire, T. Newcomb, M. Rosenberg, and P. Tannenbaum, (Eds.), *Theories of cognitive consistency: A sourcebook.* Chicago: Rand McNally, 1968.

Rosenberg, M. J. *Conceiving the self.* New York: Basic Books, 1979.

Rosenhan, D. L. On being sane in insane places. *Science,* 1973, *179,* 250–258.

Rosenshine, B. Enthusiastic teaching: A research review. *School Review,* 1970, *72,* 499–514. (a)

Rosenshine, B. Evaluation of classroom instruction. *Review of Educational Research,* 1970, *40,* 279–300. (b)

Rosenshine, B., and McGaw, B. Issues in assessing teacher accountability in public education. *Phi Delta Kappan,* 1972, *43,* 640–643.

Rosenthal, R., and Jacobson, L. *Pygmalion in the classroom: Teacher expectation and pupils' intellectual development.* New York: Holt, Rinehart & Winston, 1968. (a)

Rosenthal, R., and Jacobson, L. Teacher expectations for the disadvantaged. *Scientific American,* 1968, 218(4), 19–23. (b)

Rothbart, M., Dalfen, S., and Barrett, R. Effects of teacher's expectancy on student–teacher interaction. *Journal of Educational Psychology,* 1971, *62,* 49–54.

Rowe, M. B. Reflections on wait-time: Some methodological questions. *Journal of Research in Science Teaching,* 1974, *11*(3), 263–279. (a)

Rowe, M. B. Relation and wait-time and rewards to the development of language, logic and fate control. Part II—Rewards. *Journal of Research in Science Teaching,* 1974, *11*(4), 290–308. (b)

Rowe, M. B. Wait-time and rewards as instructional variables, their influence on language, logic, and fate-control. Part I—Wait-time. *Journal of Research in Science Teaching,* 1974, *2*(2), 81–94. (c)

Rubovits, P., and Maehr, M. Pygmalion analyzed: Toward an explanation of the Rosenthal–Jacobson findings. *Journal of Personality and Social Psychology,* 1971, *19,* 197–203.

Russell, D., Purkey, W., and Siegel, B. The artfully inviting teacher: A hierarchy of strategies. *Education,* Fall 1982, *103* (1).

Rutter, M., Maughan, B., Mortimore, P., Ouston, J., and Smith, A. *Fifteen thousand hours: Secondary schools and their effects on children.* Cambridge: Harvard University Press, 1979.

Sabine, G. A. *How students rate their schools and teachers.* Washington, D.C.: National Association of Secondary School Principals, 1971.

Saint-Exupéry, A. de. *The little prince.* New York: Harcourt, Brace & World, 1943.

Schachtel, E. G. *Metamorphosis: On the development of affect, perception, attention, and memory.* New York: Basic Books, 1959.

Scheffler, I. Philosophical models of teaching. In R. S. Peters (Ed.), *The concept of education.* London: Routledge & Kegan Paul, 1967.

Schmidt, J. J. Understanding punishment and encouraging positive discipline. *The Humanistic Educator,* in press.

Seligman, M. E. *Helplessness: On depression, development, and death.* San Francisco: W. H. Freeman, 1975.

Shavelson, R., Hubner, J., and Stanton, G. Self-concept: Validation of construct interpretations. *Review of Educational Research,* 1976, *46*(3), 407–441.

Shaw, G. B. *Pygmalion.* New York: Dodd, Mead, 1940.

Simon, S., Howe, L., and Kirschenbaum, H. *Values clarification: A handbook of practical strategies for teachers and students* (2nd ed.). New York: Hart, 1978.

Sloane, H. N. *Classroom management: Remediation and prevention.* New York: John Wiley, 1976.

Smith, B. *A tree grows in Brooklyn.* New York: Harper & Row, 1943.

Smith, M. Meta-analysis of research on teacher expectations. *Evaluation in Education,* 1980, *4,* 53–55.

Snygg, D., and Combs, A. W. *Individual behavior: A new frame of reference for psychology.* New York: Harper & Row, 1949.

Soares, A. T., and Soares, L. M. Interpersonal and self-perceptions of disadvantaged and advantaged high school students. *Proceedings of the 78th Annual Convention of the American Psychological Association,* 1970, 5(1), 457–458.

Spears, W. D., and Deese, M. E. Self concept as cause. *Educational Theory,* 1973, *23*(2), 144–153.

Stanwyck, D. J., and Felker, D. W. *Self-concept and anxiety in middle elementary school children: A developmental survey.* Paper presented at the meeting of the American Educational Research Association, Chicago, March 1974.

Sunby, D. Y. *The relationship of teacher–child perception similarities and teacher-ratings, and the effect of teachers' similarity expectancies of children's self-perceptions and teacher-rating.* Unpublished doctoral dissertation, Purdue University, 1971.

Swift, J. *Gulliver's travels.* New York: W. W. Norton, 1961.

Szasz, T. *Heresies.* Garden City, N.Y.: Anchor Books, 1976.

Tagiuri, R., Bruner, J. S., and Blake, R. R. On the relation between feelings and perception of feelings among members of small groups. In E. E. Maccoby, T. M. Newcomb, and E. L. Hartley (Eds.), *Readings in social psychology.* New York: Holt, Rinehart, & Winston, 1958.

Taylor, M. *Intercorrelations among three methods of estimating students' attention.* Stanford, Calif.: Stanford Center for Research on Teaching, 1968.

Thomas, A. *Invitational education: A framework for relating two theories to educational practice.* Paper presented at the American Educational Research Association Convention, New York, March 1982.

Tillich, P. *The courage to be.* New Haven: Yale University Press, 1952.

Tjosvold, D. Alternate organizations for schools and classrooms. In D. Bartel and L. Saxe (Eds.), *Social psychology of education: Research and theory.* New York: Hemisphere Press, 1977.

Tjosvold, D., and Santamaria, P. *The effects of cooperation and teacher support on student attitudes toward classroom decision-making.* Paper presented at the meeting of the American Educational Research Association, New York, March 1977.

Toffler, A. (Ed.). *Learning for tomorrow: The role of the future in education.* New York: Random House, 1974.

Treves, Sir F. *The Elephant man and other reminiscences.* London, England: Cassell, 1923.

Turner, R. B. *Teacher invitations and effectiveness as reported by physical education students, grades 9–12.* Paper presented at the meeting of the American Educational Research Association, New York, March 1982.

Usher, R., and Hanke, J. The "third force" in psychology and college teacher effectiveness research at the University of Northern Colorado. *Colorado Journal of Educational Research,* 1971, *10*(2), 3–10.

Wagoner, J. L., Jr. *Thomas Jefferson and the education of a new nation.* Bloomington, Ind.: Phi Delta Kappa Educational Foundation, 1976.

Wasicsko, M. M. *The effects of training and perceptual orientation on the reliability of perceptual inferences for selecting effective teachers.* Unpublished doctoral dissertation, University of Florida, 1977.

Webster, M., and Sobieszek, B. *Sources of self-evaluation: A formal theory of significant others and social influence.* New York: John Wiley, 1974.

Weir, E. C. The meaning of learning and the learning of meaning. *Phi Delta Kappan,* 1965, *46*(6), 280–284.

Wilkins, W. E., and Glock, M. D. *Teacher expectations and student achievement: A replication and extension.* Ithaca, N.Y.: Cornell University, 1973. (ERIC Document Reproduction Service No. 080-567)

Williams, R., and Kamala, A. *Cooperative classroom discipline.* Columbus, Ohio: Charles E. Merrill, 1973.

Willis, B. J. The influence of teacher expectation on teachers' classroom interaction with selected children (Doctoral dissertation, George Peabody College of Teaching, 1969). *Dissertation Abstracts International,* 1970, *30*(11-A), 5072.

Wylie, R. C. *The self-concept.* Lincoln: University of Nebraska Press, 1961.

Wylie, R. C. *The self-concept* (Vol. 1, rev. ed.). Lincoln: University of Nebraska Press, 1974.

Wylie, R. C. *The self-concept: Theory and research on selected topics* (Vol. 2, rev. ed.). Lincoln: University of Nebraska Press, 1979.

Wyne, M. D., White, K. P., and Coop, R. H. *The black self.* Englewood Cliffs, N.J.: Prentice-Hall, 1974.

Ziller, R. C. *The social self.* New York: Pergamon Press, 1973.

Zimmerman, I. L., and Allebrand, G. N. Personality characteristics and attitudes toward achievement of good and poor readers. *The Journal of Educational Research.* 1965, *59*(1), 28–30.

INDEX

Active listening, 62
Administrators, 113–117
Aggressive behavior, 82
Alberti, R. E., 81, 82
Allebrand, G. N., 29
Alice in Wonderland, 29
Allport, G. W., 22
Altman, H., 42, 56
Areas of inviting, 72–88
Aronson, E., 31
Artfully inviting, 20
Aspy, D. N., 42
Asserting, 81–83
Athletics, 110–113
Attending, 62
Attitudes, 6
Avila, D., 7, 21, 31, 51

Bachman, J. G., 27
Baker, J. P., 5
Barbe, W., 67
Barrett, R., 5
Beauty and the Beast, 4
Being-with process, 16
Behavior modification, 51
Bellack, A., 6
Bennett, A. C., 49
Bennett, J., 82
Benton, J. A., 37
Berger, P., 57
Biddle, B. J., 39
Biklen, S. K., 22
Blake, R. R., 81
Bloom, B. S., 4, 38
Blume, R. A., 22
Body language, 64
Bogdan, R. C., 12, 22
Boy, A. V., 44
Branch, C., 32, 33, 78
Braun, C., 3, 58

Brophy, J. E., 3, 5, 12, 39, 40, 61, 64, 85
Brown, C., 79
Brubaker, D., 90
Bruner, J., 81, 85
Bryan, M., 11, 13
Buber, M., 15, 16
Bugelski, B. R., 28
Buhler, J. H., 42
Burnout, 72–74
Buscaglia, L., 41
Bus drivers, 117–119
Butts, H., 80

Cafeteria, school, 105–107
Cage, B., 77
Campbell, J. R., 85
Campbell, W. W., 31
Canfield, J., 13, 62
Carlsmith, J. M., 31
Carnoy, M., 90
Carroll, L., 29
Cartwright, D. S., 79
Cassell, P., 51
Chaikin, A. L., 5, 60
Chamberlin, J. G., 25
Charles, C. M., 51
Child, I. L., 40
Children's Defense Fund of the
    Washington Research Project, 11
Childs, J. L., 39
Clark, D. H., 3
Cohen, R. D., 5
Coleman, J. S., 82
Combs, A. W., 7, 21, 22, 23, 24, 26, 31,
    36, 37, 80
Comments
    disinviting, 132
    inviting, 132
Communication
    oral, 64

Communication (continued)
    patterns, 8–9
    physical, 64
Compliments, 64
Coop, R. H., 27
Coopersmith, S., 26, 32
Coping, 85–87
Cormany, R. B., 29
Cotler, S. B., 82
Coudert, J., 73
Counselors, 119–123
Courage to Be, 45
Cousins, N., 78
Courtesy, 51
Crist, J. L., 5
Curriculum, 2, 16, 28, 46, 80, 93, 107
Curtis, J., 42
Curtis, R. C., 31

Dalfen, S., 5
Damico, S., 32, 79
Dawn Patrol, 85
DeCharms, R., 41
Deese, M. E., 29
Delega, V. J., 60
Delinquents, 79
Democracy, 42, 50
Deutsch, M., 56
Dewey, J., 15, 25, 86
Dickman, J. F., 37
Diggory, J. C., 26
Discipline, inviting approach to, 50–53
Disinvited students, 10–11, 14–15
Disinviting comments, 132
Disinviting message, 5
Disruptive student, 33, 52
Doing with, 39
Dollar, B., 51
Dorland's Illustrated Medical Dictionary, 3
Dowaliby, F. J., 62
Doyle, W., 3
Dreikurs, R., 51
Drugger, C. W., 42
Dumas, A., 32

Edeburn, C. E., 29
Edelwich, J., 72

Efficacy, professional, 6–7
Efficient factory, 90–92
Efficient factory school, 92–94
Elementary school, 102–105
Elephant Man, 39
Egan, G., 62
Elias, P., 5
Elkind, D., 86
Emmons, M. L., 81, 82
Environment
    disinviting physical, 134
    efficient factory, 90–92
    efficient factory school, 92–94
    inviting family, 94–96
    inviting family school, 96–98
    inviting physical, 56–57, 134
Epstein, J. L., 90
Epstein, S., 27
Evertson, C. M., 3, 5, 61, 64
Expectations, positive, 97

Factory model school, 92–94
Fagan, M., 64
Faith and History, 46
Family model school, 96–98
Farina, A., 4
Felice, L. G., 4
Felker, E. W., 27, 29, 62
Field, J., 51
Fielder, W. R., 5
Findley, W., 11, 13
Finney, S., 5
Fishell, K. N., 36
Fisher, R., 67
Fiore, Q., 25
Fitts, W. H., 26
Flanders, J. P., 3
Florida Key, 77–87
Food-service professionals, 105–107
Frericks, A. H., 12
Friedman, H., 40
Friedman, P., 4
Fromm, E., 40

Garber, J., 22
Gaudry, E., 82, 83
Gerber, T., 20, 90
Gergen, K. J., 27

Giorgi, A., 36
Glock, M. D., 5, 30
Goldberg, M. L., 84
Good, T. L., 3, 5, 6, 12, 39, 40, 85
Gooding, C. T., 37
Gordon, T., 62
Grant, B. M., 64
Graves, W. H., 77, 78, 90
Greene, D., 41
Gregory, D., 13
Grouping, 11–13
Guerra, J. J., 82
Gulliver's Travels, 81

Haan, R. F., 31
Hall, E. T., 39
Hamner, W. T., 26
Hancock, G., 3
Hanke, J., 37, 42
Hansen, J. C., 27
Haskins, J., 80
Helplessness, learned, 22, 82
Hennings, D. G., 64
Herbert, C., 56
Hinde, R. A., 28
Hobbs, N., 11
Hockaday, L., 49
Holmes, D., 51
Holmes, M., 51
Hook, S., 86
House, P., 61
Howe, L., 82
Hubner, J., 29
Humanistic Education, 55
Hunt, J. M., 38
Hyman, R., 6

Iatrogenic diseases, 3
Individual Behavior, 22
Inglis, S. C., 4
Insel, P., 39, 61
Intentionality, 45
Intentionally disinviting, 17–18
Intentionally inviting, 19–20
Internal dialogue, 42–43
Investing, 83–85
Inviting
    administrators, 113–117

areas, 72–88
bus drivers, 117–119
choices, 47–50
comments, 132
counselors, 119–123
elementary school, 102–105
family, 94–96
family school, 96–98
food-service professionals, 105–
    107
message, 4
middle school, 107–110
oneself, personally, 72–74
oneself, professionally, 76–77
others, personally, 74–78
others, professionally, 77–87
physical educators, 110–113
secondary-school teachers, 126–
    129
secretaries, 123–126
skills, 55–70
Invitational education
    definition, 2
    derivation, 2–3
    development, 3
Invitations
    accepting, 49–50
    ensuring delivery, 65–66
    following through, 69
    limited time, 65
    making attractive, 64–65
    sending, 48–49
Irwin, F. S., 32
Ivey, A. E., 45

Jacobson, L., 5, 39, 61
James, W., 15, 22
Jefferson, T., 42
Jersild, A. T., 30, 31
Jones, S. C., 39
Jourard, S. M., 1, 16, 22, 37, 58, 75
Joyce, B., 76

Kamala, A., 51
Kegan, R., 22, 27
Kelley, H. H., 27
Kelly, G. A., 22, 84
Kesey, K., 4

Kifer, E., 3
Killer statements, 13
King Lear, 62
Kiraly, J., 80
Kirschenbaum, H., 82
Kliebard, H., 6
Knowles, J. H., 73
Koffman, R. G., 37
Kohlberg, L., 82
Kraft, A., 59
Kranz, P. L., 36

Labeling, 11–13
Lambeth, C. R., 4, 72
Landry, R. G., 29, 42
Langley, N., 38
Lasch, C., 87
Learned helplessness, 22, 82
Learning, as a function of self-concept, 77–87
Learning for Tomorrow, 89
Lecky, P., 22, 26
Lee, H., 62
Lefcourt, H. M., 82
Lepper, M. R., 41
Levels of functioning
    intentionally disinviting, 17–18
    intentionally inviting, 19–20
    unintentionally disinviting, 18
    unintentionally inviting, 18–19
Levin, D., 52
Leviton, H., 80
Lewis, H. G., 90
Liebman, J., 72
Lifton, W., 44
Limited time invitation, 65
Lippitt, R., 41
"Little Orphant Annie", 51
Little Prince, 36
Luckman, T., 57

Maehr, M., 39, 41
Mahoney, M. J., 41, 43
Manchild in the Promised Land, 79
Manning, J., 51
Maslow, A., 45
Masters, E. L., 49
Maughan, B., 5

May, R., 45
Maynard, P. E., 27
McDonald, F., 5
McGaw, B., 90
McLuhan, M., 25
McPartland, J. M., 90
Mead, G. H., 22
"Meaning of Learning and the Learning of Meaning", 71
Mehrabian, A., 59
Meichenbaum, D., 43
Mendels, G. E., 3
Metamorphosis, 83
Mettee, D. R., 31
Michaels, F., 57
Middle school, 107–110
Miller, S. I., 85
Minority-group student, 80
Mizer, J. E., 10
Moore, T. W., 50
More, A., 61
Mortimore, P., 5
Motivation, 31
Moustakas, C. E., 40

Negotiations, 66–67
Net, 45
Newman, A. J., 22
Niebuhr, R., 46
Nigger, 13
Noad, B. M., 42
Nonverbal behavior, 5, 63
Notz, W. W., 42
Novak, J. M., 82

O'Mally, P. M., 27
On Golden Pond, 18
One Flew over the Cuckoo's Nest, 4
O'Roark, A. M., 37
Ouston, J., 5
Owen, E. H., 78

Panitch, D., 39
Patterson, C. H., 26, 38, 55
Perception
    basis of behavior, 23–24
    defined, 24
    intellectual tradition, 22–23

Perception (continued)
    learning of, 24
    reflected upon, 25
    teacher, 36–44
Personal behaviors
    disinviting, 133
    inviting, 133
Peace of Mind, 72
Phares, E. J., 82
Physical educators, 110–113
Pine, G. J., 44
Plum, A., 56
Policy, 2, 13, 16, 28, 46, 96, 107
Pomerance, B., 39
Positive expectations, 97
Positive self-regard, 31, 32–33
Powers, T., 22
Praise, 64–65
Professional efficacy, 6–7
Professionally inviting
    oneself, 76–77
    others, 77–78
Pullias, E. V., 36
Punishment, 52
Purkey, W. W., 21, 27, 31, 32, 47, 51,
    57, 77, 90
Pygmalion, 25
Pygmalion in the Classroom, 5

Raimy, V. C., 26
Reading behavior backwards, 62
Reis, R., 80
Rejection, 67–69
Relating, 78–81
Respect, 45–46
Richard III, 51–52
Richards, A. C., 22, 62
Richards, F., 22, 62
Riley, J. W., 51
Rist, R. C., 3, 11, 12
Rogers, C. R., 3, 22, 26, 35, 62, 75
Rosenberg, M. J., 27, 32, 33
Rosenhan, D. L., 4
Rosenshine, B., 61, 90
Rosenthal, R., 5
Rothbart, M., 5
Rowe, M. B., 64, 65, 84–85

Rubovits, P., 39
Russell, D., 57
Rutter, M., 5
Ryerson, F., 38

Sabine, G. A., 59
Saint-Exupéry, 36
Santamaria, P., 41
Schachtel, E. G., 83
Scheffler, I., 43
Schmidt, J. J., 51
Schumer, H., 62
School
    cafeteria, 105–107
    efficient factory, 92–94
    inviting family, 96–98
    suspension, 11
Schwartz, H., 79
Secondary-school teachers, 126–129
Secretaries, 123–126
Self-concept
    development, 26–29
    as guidance system, 29–31
    positive self-regard, 86
    situation-specific, 78
    theory, 25–26
Self-disclosure, 60
Self-fulfilling prophecy, 6
Self-regard, positive, 31, 32–33
Seligman, M., 22, 82
Shakespeare, W., 42, 51–52, 62
Shavelson, R., 29
Shaw, G. B., 25
Siegel, B., 10, 57, 72
Sigler, E., 5
Significant others, 27
Signs
    disinviting, 135
    inviting, 135
Simon, S., 82
Sloane, H. N., 51
Smith, A., 5
Smith, B., 96
Smith, F., 6
Smith, M., 3
Snygg, D., 22, 23, 26, 31
Soares, A. T., 40
Soares, L. M., 40

Sobieszek, B., 27
Soper, D. W., 37
Spargur, J., 27
Spears, W. D., 29
Spielberger, D. C., 82–83
Spoon River Anthology, 49
Stance, teacher, 44–47
Stanton, G., 29
Stanwyck, D. J., 29
Stapleton, M., 49
Stillion, J., 64
Student
    attitudes, 6
    disinviting, 10
    disruptive, 33, 52
    minority group, 80
    perceived as able, 38–39
    perceived as responsible, 40–42
    perceived as valuable, 39–40
    perception of self, 77
    self-regard, 86
    suspension, 11
Sunby, D. Y., 27
Suspension, student, 11
Swift, J., 81
Systematic extinction, 10
Szasz, T., 32

Tagiuri, R., 81
Taylor, M., 63
Taylor, S., 12
Teacher
    attitudes, 3, 4, 5
    behavior, 47–48
    expectations, 3, 5–6
    perception, 36–44
    perception of education, 43–44
    perception of self, 42–43
    stubborn, 19–20
Teacher stance
    definition, 44
    qualities of, 44–47
Technology, 91–92, 93–94
Testing, 93
Theory of practice, 2, 36, 44, 50
Thomas, A., 43

Three Musketeers, 32
Tillich, P., 45
Tjosvold, D., 41
Toffler, A., 89
To Kill a Mockingbird, 62
Tomson, B., 79
Totheroh, D., 85
"Tragedy", 27
Transparent Self, 58
Tree Grows in Brooklyn, 96
Trust, 58–60
Turiel, E., 82
Turner, R. B., 3, 4
Two Gentlemen of Verona, 42

Unintentionally disinviting, 18
Unintentionally inviting, 18–19
Usher, R., 37, 42
Ury, W., 67

Wagoner, J. L., 42
Wait-time, 5, 84–85
Wasicsko, M. M., 3, 36, 37, 44
Wass, H. L., 22
Weber, W. A., 36
Webster, M., 27
Weil, M., 76
Weir, E. C., 71
Wells, H., 13, 62
White, K. P., 27
White, R., 41
Wilkins, W. E., 5
Williams, R., 51
Willis, B. J., 5, 10
Withness, 46
Wizard of Oz, 38, 98–99
Woolf, E. A., 38
Working with Groups, 44
Wylie, R, C., 4, 26
Wyne, M. D., 27

Zanna, M. P., 31
Zellner, M., 90
Ziller, R. C., 32
Zimmerman, I. L., 29